G000255092

CHAMPIONSHIP MATCH FISHING

CHAMPIONSHIP MATCH FISHING
Ten of the Best

CLIVE SMITH

DAVID & CHARLES
Newton Abbot   London   North Pomfret (Vt)

British Library Cataloguing in Publication Data

Smith, Clive
  Championship match fishing: ten of the best.
  1. Tournament fishing
  I. Title
  799.1'1   SH455.2

ISBN 0-7153-8252-7

Typeset by Typesetters (Birmingham) Limited
and printed in Great Britain
by Biddles Limited, Guildford, Surrey
for David & Charles (Publishers) Limited
Brunel House Newton Abbot Devon

Published in the United States of America
by David & Charles Inc
North Pomfret Vermont 05053 USA

Contents

I should like to thank Gordon Holland for his help in preparing the book, John Sheward for the drawings, and all those who kindly supplied the photographs.

1

The Embassy Challenge

It was in 1968 that one of the most significant developments affecting the future of match fishing came with the introduction of the sport's first big sponsored event. This was warmly welcomed by anglers all over the country as a much needed shot-in-the-arm for an activity which previously had been somewhat neglected in the promotional field.

Not surprisingly, this competition, then known as the NFA Knockout, was accompanied by all the excitement and razza-matazz which has now become a regular part of our more important events. It was sponsored by the *People* and *Angler's Mail*—still the only major angling backing to emerge from Fleet Street.

After two years the event was taken over by Wills when the first change of name was made, to the Woodbine Challenge. Later it became the Embassy Challenge, the name by which it is known today.

Fortunately for the sport and the future of sponsored events the initial match, in 1968, was a big success. It was won by one of the top anglers in the country, Kevin Ashurst, of Leigh, Lancashire, which is always a boost for any event; and, probably of equal significance, he landed a big catch, more than thirty pounds of handsome bream.

With ingredients like this, the future of the match looked secure, a happy state of affairs for the 20,000-or-so anglers who were competing in these early years. It was also particularly fortunate for me as in the following year I was to enjoy an excellent run in the event and, just as important, gain experience of this completely new matchfishing dimension, which whetted my appetite for the years ahead.

As the original title indicated, the match is organised on a knock-out basis involving a series of rounds at varying levels and culminating in a grand final with equal numbers of competitors drawn from eight regions of the country.

The match structure has changed only slightly since its inception. Then the first round was at club level, progressing to association and then regional rounds, with the last ten qualifiers from each area going through to the grand final.

Nowadays the first club round has been dispensed with but competitors still have to overcome the association round, then the regional final, to reach the big decider. This change was undoubtedly adopted in order to make the event thoroughly professional in view of the large amounts of prize money involved, though to the best of my knowledge the competition has always enjoyed a clean bill of health.

In the early years it was not much of a problem to get through the club-level first round from which 10 per cent of the entry progressed. There was no limit to the number of tickets any angler could purchase and the sport, through the national body, obviously derived increasing benefit according to the size of the entries.

I recall well our club-level contests, extremely pleasant evening affairs in idyllic surroundings. They were held at a local still-water venue, Hewell Grange, a former stately home built for Clive of India. More recently, though, Hewell has been used as a remand centre—who says crime doesn't pay?

Imagine the balmy, early-season evenings with the hum of the dragonflies, fishing from the colourful bank of the pool, well lined with an abundance of rhododendron bushes. This was the setting we enjoyed each week until one of the qualifying tickets was secured.

After a match there would be a visit to the local hostelry where the winner would buy drinks while those less successful would discuss tactics for the following week. From this it can be imagined that the pressure at this stage of the competition was far from great. Usually it took around five to seven pounds of perch and roach to secure a qualifying weight, and it was a catch of less than six pounds which saw me through to my association round in 1969. But that next stage of the competition, at association level, held on the prolific BAA waters of the Severn at Severn Stoke, about ten miles below Worcester, was a more serious affair.

There were 130 club qualifiers in the line-up, and as with the first round, 10 per cent were to go through to the regional fish-off. This meant that I had to gain a place in the top thirteen.

The venue was really first class for this type of match and the options open to competitors were enormous. In fact, I can't think of a fish swimming in our English freshwaters which does not hold residence on this particular stretch, and quite a few of them are in matchwinning quantities. For example, it would be possible to win with a chub or roach catch which could be achieved with hemp seed or tare baits. But the favourite of them all to secure top spot would be a catch mainly of bream.

Now while these species are a pleasure to fish for in terms of angling technique, my aim was purely to qualify so the fish I selected was the more humble bleak. From pre-match assessment it seemed impossible to select a peg which could not produce six or seven pounds of bleak in the allowed five-hour period. And as this was just another rung of the ladder up to the grand final, I was not looking for any sensational catch, but more of a safe bet.

In those pre-pole days my plan was to fish with a rod and reel together with a piece of hardwood secured some three feet from the hook. This is shaped similarly to an Arlesey bomb, only slightly longer, about two-and-a-half inches, and not quite so wide as the average bomb (see Fig 1). It is left unpainted to allow it to absorb water. This has the advantages of increasing the casting weight considerably, and giving a much lower profile in the water, and increases stability when the wind creates choppy conditions.

Whipped on to the end of the hardwood bomb is a ring which is simply tied on to the reel line. I used 2½lb breaking-strain line, obviously not because of the size of the fish, but because it is very much easier to see in difficult conditions.

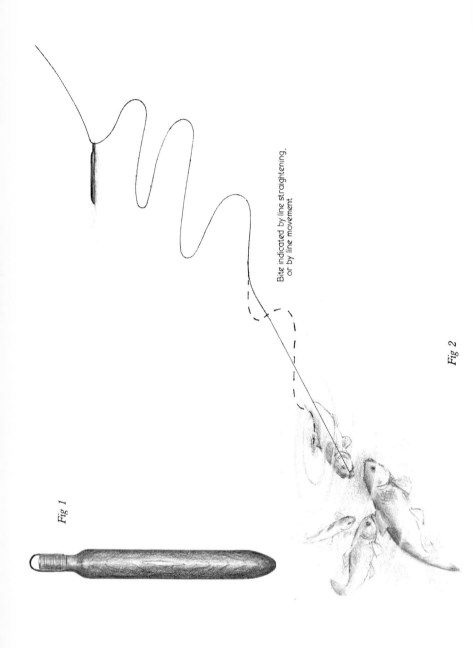

Fig 1

Bite indicated by line straightening,
or by line movement

Fig 2

With this bleak-fishing set-up I used a 1lb hooklength with size 18 or 20 small barbed hook, and a single maggot, not too large, as bait. The line is completely free of shots and simply left to float on the surface. The weight of the bait and hook submerges the business end a couple of inches, and bite indication is given by the quick straightening out of the line as the fast-moving bleak takes the bait (see Fig 2).

Feed comprises a little of everything for bleak, which love to sort through a selection of 'goodies'. My menu often consists of a few floaters, some crushed, a couple of handfuls of pinkies, a few squatts, bits of sawdust and a handful of dried groundbait. Very few large maggots are included.

Feeding varies according to the catch rate, being fairly regular when sport is slow, using quantities sufficient to cover a 10p piece, but far less often, perhaps every tenth cast, when I am catching well.

To achieve a smooth rhythm I simply set the hook in line with my free hand so that every retrieved fish arrives exactly in that position, ignoring the reel completely.

I found this to be ideal for starters, when a few suicidal fish could be taken at a rod-length's distance from the bank, but very often a larger sample of bleak could be caught by gaining an extra rod length out. For this tactic, the rhythm is maintained by operating the surplus line between the butt ring and the reel.

On retrieving the tackle from this more distant position the free hand simply takes hold of the line, and with a slow, easy pull takes up the surplus, at the same time lifting the rod to a vertical position. Assuming that the bait is still usable, a gentle flick re-positions the terminal tackle in the water, at the same time releasing the surplus line.

When a fish is contacted exactly the same procedure is followed with the free hand, but because the surplus line would be a disadvantage if let loose, it is trapped by the reel finger against the rod, the fish removed from the hook, and the cast made as previously.

In fishing this method, the angler's working position depends on cover available at his swim. If this is ample, then fish will move in very close for long periods and the angler can frequently get away with a sitting-down posture which has the advantage of creating a lower profile and alarms the fish less. On the more open pegs a standing position is greatly preferred to facilitate lengthier casts, even though the angler is more obvious.

In the NFA Knockout Match I drew a peg upstream of Severn Stoke Lane, a stretch where trees had been removed only a short time before, leaving anglers to fish from boulders which had been used for revetment. It was certainly not the most comfortable of fishing stations, but that is the luck of the draw.

It was bright and sunny, when I could well have done with a little cover, but being a match angler I had become well used to accepting the peg which I had drawn.

I just got on with the job, and it was really as pleasant a match as I could have expected in the circumstances, probably made easier by the fact that my particular area was not highly rated for species other than bleak and there was therefore little distraction from my fellow competitors.

Funnily enough, the bleak I was catching were quite large, though they became increasingly scarce towards the end of the match, and never really moved in such a quantity as to make me break out in a sweat.

My final catch weight was 7lb 3½oz and this put me sixth within the 130-competitor field. It was satisfying inasmuch as I could well have chased rainbows in this otherwise non-productive area if I had tried to catch larger fish, and might easily have failed. The result meant that I had read the match correctly and I even finished with the top weight in that upstream area.

Below the Lane, from the well-fancied bushes section, Coleshill ace Norman Hayes won the match with 13lb 2oz of bream which fell to breadflake bait. Norman was justified in going for bream in that area as it was well known for its abundance.

Having cleared this first really major hurdle, the next challenge was the regional final. In 1969 this was hosted by the giant Worcester Association who selected for the match course their 'blue riband' waters in the Beauchamp Court area.

Quite obviously, standards improved and competition became tougher with each round. At regional level quite a big percentage of the entry, given a fair chance, could reasonably expect to qualify for the ten places in the grand final.

It was therefore essential that in preparing for the match, a lot of homework had to be done. It was critical that correct methods and tactics were decided upon because if a competitor went off on the wrong track there would be no chance of changing course in mid-match. The quality of the field would be far too good to allow this. Many would read the signs perfectly and be well on the way to a qualifying weight after two-and-a-half hours of the five-hour encounter.

For me, this pre-match build-up was similar to a punter studying form for a big race. It soon became clear that the vital question was going to surround the qualifying weight needed for the tenth and last place. Then, having assessed a figure through arduous study of contest results on the selected length, it was equally important that the required catch had to be aimed for with minimal risk.

The water was noted for big chub and bream—there were only odd barbel there in those days and these could be discounted. Despite the abundance of big fish there was no guarantee that they would be feeding along the full course of the match length. True, it was a safe bet that one of these species was going to provide the winning weight, largely because most competitors would be fishing for them.

Having succeeded in the previous round with bleak, I suppose I was a bit biased in deciding to make these tiny silver fish my target again in this match. I worked out the qualifying weight for tenth place at six to seven pounds and was encouraged by the fact that in some ten bleak matches over the previous two years I had averaged about nine pounds, the important factor here being consistency.

My lowest weight of bleak in big open events such as the

Severn Championship and BAA Welfares had been around seven pounds. I was helped in making my decision by the curious approach of many anglers in those days who chose to treat bleak as a species not worthy of attention.

My decision made, the three weeks between the association round and the regional final saw me keeping very much in touch with the bleak situation. Very often after a week-end match I would slip off to a bleak water and pass the last couple of hours of daylight happily catching one after another.

These were, of course, the pre-pole days, and my set-up was the same as for the previous round, a method which I am becoming increasingly convinced is still as effective as anything else, poles included.

On match day, Saturday, 30 August, I was thoroughly confident of catching a qualifying weight and the draw wasn't bothering me to any real degree. I would obviously have liked a peg with a bit of cover, but I approached the match in a really wonderful state of mind.

Then the worst happened when, ironically, I drew a peg in an extremely good area; good for chub and bream, that is, rather than for bleak. A lower-rated draw would have left me much more confident, in view of my match plan, and the fact that I had chosen a noted area served only to add extra pressure with the knowledge that there were numbers of large fish to be caught. A mediocre draw would have left me with a clear approach in my mind!

On my upstream flank was Colin Clough, at that time a successful and well-known match angler who gained a lot of repute in that epic battle on the Sedgemoor Drain with Dave Burr, when he finished runner-up. In addition to many other match successes, he had also gained the Welland Championship title. He, too, had a good draw for big fish, a position which suited him well. And just to make things doubly difficult, the man pegged above Colin Clough was no lesser matchman than Norman Hayes. He had a fine reputation, especially on the Midland circuit, and had actually finished third in the previous year's NFA Knockout grand final at Coombe Abbey Lake. Also well known for his big-fish style, Norman was obviously thinking that this was a lucky match in which to be involved!

In no time at all I was attempting to regain my earlier pleasant mental state and tried to anticipate how the match was going to go. On looking back, I can see clearly the picture which I had formed, and it is with much satisfaction I reflect that, with the limited experience I had at the time, I was so correct in my assessment.

It was quite obvious that the area which I had drawn was going to produce more than its fair share of qualifiers. Added to this was the fact that two of the best anglers in the business were situated immediately upstream of me, and well within my vision. In those circumstances, the approach which I planned was similar to a horse running in blinkers. I had to ignore completely the happenings around me and involve myself 100 per cent in attaining my target weight!

As the match got under way I settled into my planned bleak-fishing approach, feeding the swim with a concoction of old and new maggots, with quantities of roughage which bleak find so interesting. It wasn't long before I was catching fish at a fairly steady rate. The father of that well-known matchman of the time, Lloyd Davies, was sitting behind me and he timed my catch-rate at around ninety fish an hour.

Severn bleak aren't small, and I seemed to be well on course for a good qualifying weight. But as so often happens when bleak fishing, the pace started to slow after about three hours when I estimated that I had about seven pounds in the net. This was what I had forecast would be near to the qualifying weight at the end of the match.

Now with bleak far less prolific, I had to decide whether to continue pursuing them, or to try and catch the larger species which had obviously been accepting bait which had been missed by the small surface-feeders.

In view of the target I had set myself, it was not a difficult decision to make. I decided to keep to bleak and that meant chasing those remaining in the area about the swim, which is where the rod and reel came in extremely useful.

But during those last two hours, when I was catching at a much slower pace, I was faced with a couple of problems. For the first time in the match I became conscious of Colin and Norman catching chub. This made it very hard for me to continue the fishing for bleak which was seeming so fruitless in the latter stages of the match.

Several times I had to convince myself that my carefully thought-out plan was still working and that accommodation had been made for five or six larger weights of fish, which was how the match seemed to be going.

Nonetheless I struggled through the last hour of the match and when eventually I put my fish on the scales they took the dial round to 8lb 15½oz. My upstream rivals, Colin and Norman, both returned low double figures and finished among the first three. My score was good enough for fifth place, my plan had worked perfectly, and I was on my way to the grand final at Coombe Abbey Lake.

The Coombe Abbey final was set for Saturday, 20 September, which left me plenty of time for practice, some five weeks in fact. But I was going to need every minute I had because the venue, an out-and-out bream water, was far different from the type which in those days I had been accustomed to fishing. In fact, it was a swing-tipper's delight, a method which I had used very little indeed. Most of my bream fishing had been carried out on the lower reaches of the Severn and the Warwickshire Avon. This demanded heavy groundbaiting in the fast waters, with the incorporation of a quiver-tip rod as a means of bite detection.

Preparations for this 1969 final were made a lot easier for me in the initial stages by help from my great angling friend of those days, Lloyd Davies. He had finished fifth in the previous year's final and I had been fortunate enough to practise with him for that particular match. But as it was on untried water on those occasions, my attack had been with a float, fishing mainly for roach.

However, Lloyd was able to feed me much information and advice from knowledge gained in that final, which had been monopolised by bream.

I was thus in the position of having seen the water, though not fishing it correctly, and having had the successful method explained to me by a competitor in that event.

It wasn't long before I made my first trip to Coombe. I remember it very well: it was a Sunday-morning visit, not entailing a match but merely a practice session. With me was Tony Reece, a more skilful bream angler than myself (especially in those days), who came along to give what assistance he could.

We had to walk from the access for what seemed like miles before we came to the first available pegs, or, to be more precise, the first available peg and a half! This was what we had to settle for on that crowded, but exciting-looking water. The advantage of the public bank at Coombe is that the farther you walk the better the pegs become, so there is some recompense for the long trek.

We both fished swing-tip style at a distance of about thirty yards from the bank, and I believe we worked with size 16 hooks to 1½lb length with an Arlesey bomb 3ft from the hook, with 2½lb reel line.

To describe my groundbaiting as crude at that time would be more than fair. It was one area where big improvements had to be made. Feeding was by hand in those days and I made the big mistake of making my groundbait balls very hard in order to achieve the throwing distance required.

We finished the session with six to seven pounds of fish, and, upon analysis of the day's working, it was clear that, in addition to groundbaiting, casting and terminal tackle also needed to be improved drastically. However, after another couple of visits to the water there was a big advancement on all fronts, and I was managing to take catches well into double figures.

In 1969 the size of fish at Coombe was generally smaller than it is these days. There were good numbers around the ten- to twelve-ounce mark, and, as the private bank holding the larger specimens was not going to be used for this final, these smaller fish were going to play an important part.

Match day arrived and it was really lovely—though not necessarily for fishing. There was glorious sunshine and blue skies . . . could it make for low weights? Yet it didn't seem all that important as the atmosphere was electric. What a beautiful setting it was, I thought, for my first really big match, and the sport's only major sponsored event.

Television personalities were there to help with commentating, and 'supremo' for the day was the late Bernard Donovan, then President of Coventry DAA; what a helpful man he was.

From analysis of anglers' catches at Coombe during the run-up to the final, it seemed obvious that an area known as the lawn stretch was the favourite, which all eighty competitors would want to draw. This involved the long walk mentioned earlier; nearly all the pegs beyond the overflow, and through the wood, were being tipped as likely winners, with the end ten swims getting the casting votes. On this assessment it was thought that the best numbers to draw were between 1 and 20. But when the selection was made in alphabetical order I realised that Smith was not the best of names to have.

It was very disillusioning to watch all the low numbers being drawn as I waited for my turn. When it finally came there were only five pegs left, and they included just one of the sought-after numbers. I didn't get it, and my enthusiasm took a knock when I pulled Peg 67. Then an announcer tried to comfort us seemingly less fortunate competitors by advising all those at the high-numbered pegs not to be too disappointed as there had been a thirteen-pound carp caught in that area. I think he must have been a non-angler working from pre-fed information!

Each competitor had to walk to his peg, and unfortunately as was my habit in those inexperienced days, I had loads of everything! This included a good twenty pounds of dry groundbait, over a gallon of maggots and an equal quantity of squatts with accompanying sand.

We were, fortunately, allowed a caddie, and Ken Rollings, a

noted Coventry angler, picked up my tackle. That was the day's first stroke of luck for me because Ken was well known as a Coombe specialist; on arriving at my peg he told me not to be too disappointed as he had known good bags of fish to be taken from the area, thirteen pegs along from the access point.

The water was about three- to four-feet deep, fairly average for all the lake which at this point tends to be narrow, probably less than sixty yards across.

I was tackled up and well ready long before the start of this 1969 NFA Knockout final. On glancing about, I had never before seen so many spectators at a contest. I had to admit I was feeling a little nervous in facing up to what was after all not really my style of fishing.

Eventually the maroon indicated the commencement of the match and, as planned, I threw in four balls of groundbait, each the size of an apple and containing a fair sprinkling of squatts. I was quite pleased with the accuracy of my throw because this had been a big weakness in practice. But by then not only had my groundbait improved in texture and my baiting in positioning, but also my terminal tackle had been adjusted to suit the job in hand. My 'tail' had been extended to 4½ft with a 10in lead link holding a ¾oz bomb, and my hook was a size 18 to 1½lb bs. Admittedly an 18 is not small by today's standards, but in those days it was looked upon as tiny by the West Midlands angler more used to catching chub and big bream in moving water.

I might well have caught the very first fish in the match for after only two minutes I latched on to a roach of two to three ounces. And my second bite came shortly afterwards—a bream of about ten ounces which I promptly lost while netting! This was to be my only lost fish during the contest.

At that stage my composure was good and at reasonable intervals I was soon catching bream short of the pound. Then just as we reached the two-hour mark I caught a nice fish of 2lb 5oz which was assessed separately at the end of the match as a contender for the heaviest fish trophy.

But soon after that, sport started to slow down. I had gathered around me quite a few spectators and I would be less than honest if I did not admit that I was affected by their attention. My casting had suffered a little, and looking back I realise that I slowed down my groundbaiting as I became increasingly conscious of the crowd behind me.

By then, in the distance, I could see that a large crowd had gathered behind Rotherham angler Ernie Wilde who was playing a large bream which had retreated deep into a weedbed. They told me later that, after giving the fish several minutes to emerge from the obstacle, Ernie threw a ball of groundbait towards where the fish was lying to shock it into bolting from cover. He went on to net that bream, a three-pounder, and with it that 1969 final.

I was to finish runner-up, 1lb 14oz behind, which made that ball of groundbait worth £1,500! That was the difference in prize money between us.

I collected £500 and could not have been more pleased if I had won. It was a day I shall never forget, and in this I think I am in common with any sportsman on achieving his first big success.

For the record, the result of that 1969 final was: Ernie Wilde (Swinton) 10-10-0; Clive Smith (Birmingham) 8-11-4; Richard Bowker Jnr (Leigh) 7-3-1; R. Groom (King's Lynn) 6-11-11; J. North (Newport) 6-5-8.

2
The BAA Annual

Ask any successful match angler with a few years' experience behind him to say which is his lucky event and it is odds on that he will be able to name one without any hesitation. Every matchman I know can give evidence of having enjoyed success beyond all expectations in one particular contest. It may be just a 100-peg open regularly run by a particular association or club in which for some inexplicable reason an angler manages to put together a string of first placings. But, more surprisingly, it also happens with the larger promotions in which the most a contender would normally hope for would be one good result during his career.

It is difficult to explain how an angler such as Ivan Marks managed to win the Great Ouse Championships no fewer than three times in four years, twice with weights in excess of fifty pounds, in competition with between 600 and 800 competitors. And what is more, each victory was secured from a completely different area of the match length!

Another example of this 'lucky match' puzzle involved my fishing partner, Ken Giles. He could never go wrong when he visited the Warwickshire Avon at Luddington, later designated as the 1981 World Championship venue. During one period in the 1970s he won match after match with weights well into double figures. Even when conditions were made quite atrocious by floods he was still able to find that little bit of luck needed on such days to secure yet another first place.

I have been doubly fortunate in this respect. One exceptional run was in the very popular series of Stourport Opens on the River Severn in which I once gained nine wins out of fifteen events. It seemed that every time I attended this match I could

Clive Smith playing a barbel during the 1975 BAA Annual at Atcham on the River Severn

not help but win. Yet, by a queer twist of fate, while I was having things all my own way there, try as I would, I could never get anywhere near the prize list at Luddington where Ken Giles was doing so well.

The event which really used to excite me was the mammoth 4,000-peg Birmingham Anglers' Association Annual. This match is billed as the largest in the world, and I have no reason to doubt this claim. It stretches over a tremendous distance of something like 400 miles of pegged-out banks along the Severn and Warwickshire Avon, and is likely to be won with a big catch of barbel, chub, bream, roach, or even dace. On one occasion a well-known Birmingham angler, Ted Mant, topped the list with about eighteen pounds of bleak from a Tewkesbury peg.

This was always a very sought-after match, its popularity shown by the astonishingly rapid sale of tickets. In the 1970s the whole 4,000 would be snapped up in something like forty-five minutes when they went on sale at the Association's former headquarters in Thorp Street. Postal applications were not allowed in those days so club secretaries would form a queue stretching for several hundred yards outside the building for hours on end waiting for ticket distribution to start.

After securing places in the lower ranks of the prize list, it was in 1966 that I had my first taste of real success in this contest, which is really eight sectional matches, each of 500 competitors, with the prize money allocated accordingly. The only competitor who gained rewards extra to this sectional system of pay-out was the outright winner, though in later years this was extended to include the anglers registering the top weights from both the Severn and the Avon.

It is obvious that with such a prize structure, the sights of the contenders are mostly set on a section victory, and there is always great speculation surrounding the area in which an angler is drawn.

The match tickets are numbered, 1 to 4,000, and correspond with the competitors' peg numbers. A drawn number is allocated the starting point at Mythe Farm on the Avon and from that number, the pegs follow numerically in a clockwise direction, first up the right bank of the Avon, then down on the opposite bank to join the Severn just below Tewkesbury. They then proceed upstream along the Severn's right bank, switch to the opposite side of the river at Shrewsbury, continue down to the bottom of the course and then return to Mythe Farm.

A map of the match course is prepared but this is always a closely guarded secret until the week of the event. When eventually it is published it is of no advantage to the competitor wishing to practise at the peg he has drawn because the water is always closed to participants for the whole of that week.

In the 1966 contest scrutiny of the map showed me to be pegged on the Severn, just below Worcester at Diglis, around about the area where the Teme flows into the main river. This was a good position quite capable of producing a winning weight, and my immediate reaction was to study other areas of my section which might yield equally good or even better results. I wasn't too worried about the downstream pegs. This was largely a bream area, and these fish had not been showing at all well in that particular year. The chief danger, I felt, was going to come from the sections upstream in the vicinity of Stourport and Bewdley.

On the day of the match I found myself staked nine swims above Teme mouth. I had been given sound information about the water from colleagues who fished it regularly. I knew the depth to be seven to ten feet and that it responded well to heavy groundbaiting—a far different situation to that of today.

Although not too good, the pegging was acceptable. When the starting whistle sounded my first job was to plumb the depth. I had about seven feet of water and, though not visibly fast, it was on the heavy side so I used a bulk-shotting pattern with six AAAs placed three feet from the hook. Two smaller shots were equally spread from there to the hook, the bottom one being a No 6 (see Fig 3).

My float was a balsa type which nowadays fall into the category of a pacemaker and the hook was a size 18 to 1½lb bs and 2½lb bs reel line. I worked with a 12ft rod and an open-face reel, the close-face design at that time not being anywhere near as popular as it is today.

I started to feed groundbait and maggots, but no casters which also then had not yet caught on, especially in the West Midlands. The size of the groundbait balls were frightening by today's standards, around tennis-ball dimensions, but I had plentiful supplies, some twenty pounds dry weight.

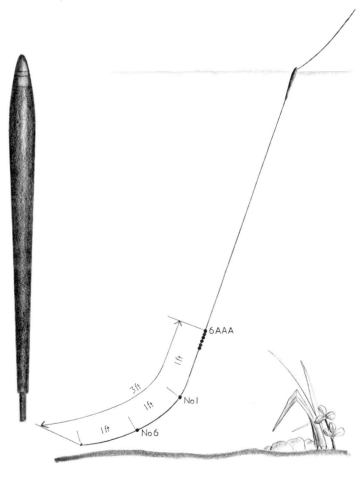

Fig 3

25

The heavy-textured balls settled quickly on the river bed and I introduced them at four- to five-minute intervals. I had my first fish after twenty minutes, a dace, then another some ten minutes later. Actually I was fishing for chub, the species for which the water was generally known, but I wasn't worried because dace very often encourage interest in the swim, thereby making chub inquisitive.

After nearly an hour, I engaged my first chub, a fish of about a pound. I had a further brace at fifteen-minute intervals, but then came a disastrous intervention. In those days the stretch was used by sea-going vessels and, sure enough, one passed through the swims at full speed. I shall never forget the name of that craft—*Wyvern H.*

The effect of these boats passing through a Lower Severn match course was effectively to kill the swims for a long period, depending on the speed of the craft and the wash it created. This also coloured the water.

It would not have been so bad from my point of view if the boat had passed through the complete section but it only covered a certain distance before finding a mooring at Worcester, thus leaving the 300 pegs upstream completely free from disturbance.

A full two hours passed before I was able to attract another bite. This was another fish around the pound mark, the general stamp for the area. The whole match was only four hours long and it meant that only thirty minutes remained for me to add to the three pounds which I had then netted.

Then sport became really hectic as I caught fish in a procession. I had one eye on my watch, dreading the final whistle which came after I had caught a further five chub. My bag totalled 9lb 13oz 12dr, but was it enough to give me first place in the 500-competitor section? I feared that one of the 300 pegs on the undisturbed water might produce more than my final weight.

As to be expected in a match of such large size, it was three or four hours before any results were available, but for me it was good news when it came: a section first. My nearest rival scaled 8lb 2oz from a peg at Stourport.

What disappointed me about this match was the fact that only just over 17½lb was needed to gain the top overall place and I had lost all that valuable time through the interruption! However, I finished seventh among the 4,000 competitors, a very satisfying result with which I won £68, quite a handsome reward in 1966.

My next achievement in this big event came four years later, in 1970. This time I drew a peg on what is known locally as the Danery Water, also on the Severn and about three miles below Bridgnorth, just above the well-known Quatford length.

This area is currently dominated by the swimfeeder, but happily in those days this was never seen. The approach was almost entirely one of float-fishing, while barbel, now found in profusion in the Middle Severn, were also largely missing. Chub were the main targets, and definitely potential matchwinners.

I was about half-way along the Danery stretch just below the big bend. I didn't rate the swim too highly; it was too deep at about thirteen feet, and slow. I would have much preferred a shallower swim, say five or six feet.

My tackle set-up was similar to that I used four years earlier, though adjusted to cope with the extra depth. But by that time groundbaiting had become more sophisticated, and, with the introduction of brown bread, a softer mix could be achieved. Also the balls had been trimmed down to about the size of an egg.

There had been a big change, too, in hookbait. The West Midlands had by then become a caster stronghold, and that was my bait on this particular day.

Casters were fished slightly differently in those early days, the general method for chub being to use them in bunches on large-size hooks, very similar to the wasp-grub approach on the Severn. There was no doubt that this caster style emerged from that particular era, though wasp grub had by then been banned as a bait.

I used a size 12 hook to a 2½lb bs trace and 3lb reel line. It was baited with three casters, and I introduced a further three to four pints of casters into the swim with the groundbait.

For the first two hours I caught chub steadily on a mid-river line, and the action soon attracted a gallery of spectators along the high bank behind me. I am convinced that this was to the detriment of the peg because after losing one very good fish it was difficult to create any new life in the swim with the observers so prominently positioned.

I went on to record a weight of 10lb 15oz, and this again secured me the top place in the section and a pay-out just short of three figures. But, although I had come out best of 500 competitors, I slipped down the overall list to seventeenth position.

In that match a lot of good weights came from the lesser-fancied sister river, the Avon, a trend to be followed for a number of years. This, I feel sure, was due to compensation water being released into the Severn on that particular week-end each year.

This was a cold discharge from Clywedog Reservoir into the Upper Severn and it chilled the river, checking sport to a marked degree immediately after its release. Following complaints from anglers an investigation was made, and as a result the release was switched from the bottom outlets of the reservoir to the warmer top layers of the dam.

This great BAA Annual was certainly proving to be a lucky contest for me for I had to wait only until the following year, 1971, for my next notable achievement. Then there was a new incentive, the introduction of a winner-take-all prize for each 1,000 pegs, this being in addition to the usual awards for the 500-competitor sections.

When the map was published I viewed my peg situation with mixed feelings. I was drawn at Grimley, on the Severn, which is some three miles upstream of Worcester. It is an area best described, especially in 1971, as a good, consistent piece of water but having little potential for any exceptional weights.

The exact location of my swim was on the upstream boundary of the Birmingham waters, about four pegs above the spinney. This was preferable to the lower reaches.

That particular year was somewhat significant for match

fishing as it was the last of the big single National Championship events before the change to a divisional structure. This match, too, was held on the Severn, not long before the BAA event.

The Birmingham team, of which I was captain, put in a lot of time practising on the national stretch, which included Grimley as the downstream section. From these visits I knew there to be a fair head of chub in the area, but the national match itself was to provide me with a much better pointer.

In this event I was staked just below Boreley, a similar water to my BAA peg and only a couple of miles upstream. A few pegs below me was Brian Lees, a well-known Northern angler from Leigh, and he recorded a very commendable weight of some twenty-five pounds which I believe took fourth place in the match. He was using a slider float and this was my cue for the BAA match.

I slightly adapted the Brian Lees tackle set-up to my own style, and then had a perfect work-out with the rig in the big Kidderminster Holiday Open in which I was also drawn at Boreley and returned a catch just short of forty pounds to clinch second place.

My float is best described as cigar shaped (see Fig 4a) with the shotting pattern as shown in Fig 4b. The drop shot is a treble A, enormous by today's standards for a bottom shot, but for some unknown reason it worked perfectly in that particular year.

The Severn had been running low during the whole of the summer and autumn, ideal conditions for the slider, and the bites were shown in either the orthodox fashion of the float submerging, or, quite often, as the fish intercepted the bottom drop shot by virtue of its size it registered an easy-to-spot lift bite.

The glass tube (see Fig 5a) which I positioned at the base of the slider was preferred to a wire ring as it offered more resistance to the fast-travelling bulk shot as they hit the bottom of the float when a strike was made.

The top eye (see Fig 5b) was 15thou diameter and positioned as near to the top as possible in order to keep the line clear of the surface and in a floating position. The reel line was 3lb bs, the hook a size 16 to 1½lb length.

Fig 4a

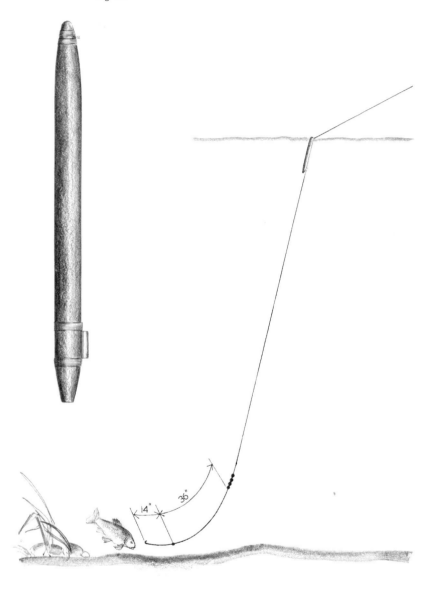

Fig 4b

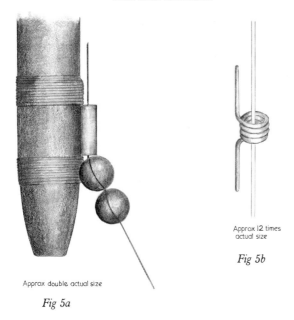

Approx 12 times
actual size

Fig 5b

Approx double actual size

Fig 5a

With casters the established bait, there was no problem about what to offer the fish, but the feeding method was still by groundbait, and in fairly large quantities too. An angler drawn on anything like a reasonable head of fish could expect to use about sixteen to eighteen pounds.

With all the information I had amassed I was in a strong position to get the best out of my BAA peg at Grimley, and as match day approached I found the event growing on me, and my enthusiasm increasing.

At last it was Sunday, 3 October 1971, and river conditions were almost identical to those which I had experienced in both the National Championships and the Kidderminster Open. It was a beautiful sunny day when I arrived at my swim with plenty of time to spare.

The pegging was generous and I had a good twenty yards though my swim was somewhat lacking in cover, this being confined mainly to tall grass and nettles along its length. I would have much preferred the next peg upstream which was fully tree-lined. I set out my stall to fish the middle of the river for the chub which I was sure were going to be there.

The coincidence of a Sunday with glorious weather was undoubtedly going to bring out the boats in large numbers with all the consequent problems. But at around 11am traffic was reasonable.

As events were to develop, similar to those in 1970, the effect of the boat traffic was going to be inconsistent in my section as part of it was above Bewdley Bridge where the river is not navigable by motor-powered craft. Competitors there were to reap the benefit of largely undisturbed water, thus giving them a definite edge on the fishing.

The match got under way and I fished double caster on the hook, feeding the swim every three or four minutes with an egg-sized ball of groundbait well laced with casters, to a mid-river line. My first chub came quite quickly, after fifteen minutes, a fish of around eight ounces and this was soon followed by a similar specimen. By the turn of the hour I was slipping smallish chub into my keepnet at regular intervals.

This pattern carried on for a couple of hours during which I had the odd larger fish nearing the pound mark. But as I had suspected boat traffic steadily increased until finally sport came to a complete standstill, and I cannot remember adding anything at all to my catch during the last ninety minutes.

Eventually I weighed in 11lb 8dr, a catch I believed to be good enough only for a place at the lower end of the prize list. I was so unenthusiastic about it, in fact, that I carried on fishing after the match, not bothering to go and find out the other results.

When the details were given to me later that evening, I had one of the biggest surprises of my matchfishing career. Not only had I secured another first place in my 500-peg section, I had been even more successful in winning the 1000-peg winner-take-all prize. It brought me a total income of £183.50, splendid reward in those days when three-figure pay-outs were few and far between. My overall position was thirteenth out of the 4,000 competitors.

In 1975 I was to make yet another sortie into the higher finishing positions, again from a peg on the Severn but this time from one of the areas furthest upstream, at Atcham. This piece of water has a fine pedigree as far as the BAA Annual is concerned, having produced several outright winning weights, plus many near misses.

Barbel were then showing in vast numbers and were widely tipped as the species required to win the event. But unfortunately there was another unpredicted rise in the river level, again attributed to compensation water. My peg was about half-a-mile below Atcham car park, and a very fast and forbidding-looking section of river it was at that point. I was not at all impressed. In fact when the match started I was 400 or 500 yards downstream viewing the favoured Tern-mouth pegs, and arrived back at my swim some fifteen minutes later.

The only way I could see of tackling the match was with a jumbo-size feeder with an increased lead weight of around two ounces. I used 8lb bs line straight through to the size 12 forged hook, and my rod was an extremely stiff two-piece nine-footer with no bite indicator at all. It was positioned almost vertically in order to keep the line well clear of the fast-running water.

I repeatedly loaded the feeder with maggots, hurling it two-thirds of the way across the river, which was some thirty-five yards wide at this point. I was somewhat surprised to catch a small (8oz) chub at a time when walking the bank seemed to be a far more attractive proposition! I viewed this catch with mixed feelings. It seemed to be the only thing keeping me, reluctantly, at my peg. Another thirty minutes went by before the rod suddenly erupted into a violent 'dance'. There was no need to strike, on the other end a 4lb barbel had skewered itself firmly. It was no mean feat getting this fish to the bank, though the 8lb line certainly had its benefits under these conditions.

This large barbel served another purpose, it was heavy enough to retain the keepnet in the water and prevent it from being washed on to dry land by the heavy stream, as had been happening.

After another fifteen or twenty minutes the incident was repeated and a similar barbel added to my catch. This happened another three times at roughly half-hour intervals. I was doing far better than I had ever dreamed of.

But then came the now-familiar check, caused by an angler who chose to fish opposite me on the other bank, also using a feeder. Sport came to an abrupt halt, and my only further action was thirty minutes from the end when I caught a slightly smaller barbel to complete my catch for that day.

I weighed in 17lb 11oz to take second place in my section of 500 and finish joint seventh in the overall field of 4,000. I was only a brace of fish away from winning this coveted title!

It was probably against the odds that I had consistently drawn pegs in this event on the River Severn, but this was to change the next year when, for the first time, I was among the contenders on the 'Cinderella' river, the Avon. My peg was at Mythe Farm, a noted downstream bream water.

On match day the Severn was more unsettled than for some years, and this opened the way for the possibility of a top catch from the Avon.

I arrived at my peg with my mind firmly made up. I was to fish for bream. The river was coloured, but not pacey, being nearly perfect for the fish I wanted to catch. The weather was overcast, and it started to rain as the match got underway—only adding further to the potential.

My gambit was to groundbait the swim with four balls consisting of a white-and-brown mix, liberally laced with equal amounts of casters and squatts. They were of tennis-ball size, introduced about two-thirds of the way across the river.

My rod was a 9½ft of quiver-tip design with a tip of 25thou and I used 2½lb line on an open-face reel with a ¾oz bomb tied to a 10in nylon link and positioned some 4½ft from my size 20 hook tied to 1½lb trace.

opposite This catch of barbel put the author well up in the prize-list in the 1975 BAA Annual

Two white gozzers were the tempters and I positioned the terminal tackle two or three yards below the point of entry of the groundbait. I had fished like this for forty-five minutes before a slow pull developed on the tip as I legered in a standing position with my rod placed on two rests—a style ideally suited to this type of bream fishing.

In this situation there is no need to rush the strike, a firm lifting of the rod is all that is required to set the hook home. This first fish was a bream around the two-pound mark.

By then the weather had become quite rough, resulting in a good ripple and, at times, waves on the water. This helped to conceal the disturbance caused by the additional balls of groundbait which I added to the swim at roughly ten-minute intervals.

I caught my second fish some twenty minutes after the first, then others followed, all around the two-pound mark, but during the third hour, for some unaccountable reason, I netted two better specimens, each of about four pounds.

At that time, too, I had another orthodox bite and with a slow lift of the rod engaged a further fish of similar size. But alas, after playing it for a couple of minutes, the hook pulled free.

By the time the final whistle sounded I had caught about a dozen bream and three roach. Together they scaled 23lb 11oz. But I was beaten only six pegs downstream by Tony Reece, the angler who had assisted me in my preparations for the NFA Knockout final at Coombe Abbey in 1969.

Tony's catch was very similar to mine but weighed just 1lb 11oz more. To make things worse, he was the competitor I most feared in my location as a first-class bream angler.

As I already knew I was second among only six pegs, there was no nail-biting tension, waiting for the results in terms of a possible first place. But when I did receive the final details, to say I was disappointed would be a gross understatement. Tony had won the match and I had finished third, beaten for second place by a mere ounce! The loss of that fish some ninety minutes from the end had robbed me of the opportunity of winning the world's largest contest.

3

The Ladbroke Championships

The Ladbroke is one of the most sought-after and prestigious titles in the whole country. In this the organisers select a line-up of top match material and site them at a venue which is undoubtedly our most prolific water under contest conditions—the noted Crown Meadow stretch of the Warwickshire Avon at Evesham which extends each side of Jubilee Bridge.

Because of the sponsors' business as bookmakers the field for this classic is guaranteed to be the best and contain all the big names on the match circuit. Ladbrokes would have little interest in running the event with any other than household names as the competitors must be attractive to the public as betting mediums.

The Evesham venue has a glittering record for this type of event and has yet to produce a winning catch of less than double figures. Also it can cater for large numbers of spectators, previous gates having reached the 10,000 mark. Yet, despite the consequent disturbance of fishing, match returns are exceptional and are unlikely to be equalled anywhere else in the country.

The 1978 line-up comprised eighteen top names, including England's World Championship squad for that year, with the country's most in-form competitors making up the number.

It was a two-tier match which meant that to become the Ladbroke champion a competitor had to win two separate contests, the first one taking the form of an eliminator. For this the eighteen competitors were drawn into groups of three with the winner from each group going forward to the second contest, the main decider. Each match was 2½-hours long and pegged on different lengths of the Evesham course.

The author in action during the 1978 Ladbroke Championships (*Angling Times*)

The morning qualifier was staked from just above the slipway some two-hundred yards upstream of Evesham bridge down to a point some six swims above the Isbourne, a small river tributary.

I was drawn right at the bottom end and my rivals in the section were double Gladding Masters champion John Wilkinson, of Elthorne, and Robin Harris, former winner of both the World Championship and First Division National titles, of Peterborough. I had the upstream peg, No 1, Robin was next at No 2 with John Wilkinson at the bottom of the section at Peg 3.

For the next 2½ hours, then, this was the only stretch of water in which I was interested. I did have time to view all three pegs, and decided there was little to choose between them, apart from the fact that the bottom swim, being the very last in the whole match, would have the normal advantage associated with all end pegs.

Of our section of three swims, mine was the shallowest, about four feet and basically it would be a one-method swim because of a large pandock bed along its front and continuing downstream for some eight or ten yards. This stretched some two-and-a-half rod lengths out from the bank and, although the pandocks could easily be missed and the swim fished with a stick float, this method could bring the problem of hooked fish simply running straight back at me, heading for the cover which they knew to be there.

Although I did set up a stick-float rig, I had little intention of using it in this first eliminating match. To me, the obvious method was the waggler, fished well over towards the far bank and cast in a downstream position in order to take advantage of a large willow tree which was situated some ten yards down the swim.

On my downstream flank, Robin's peg was deeper, some five to six feet and if anything he had a little more cover in the far-bank position. Also he had the facility of an inside swim as there was no bed of pandocks to frustrate him. But as this was an August match, on a particularly warm day as well, I felt that my shallower swim compensated for the more varied facilities which Robin had to take advantage of.

At the bottom of the section, John Wilkinson's peg was deeper still, but he had the best cover across at the far bank where the water depth decreased to about three or four feet. His inside swim was about eight feet, but, being a bright day, the danger I could see from this peg was that the bigger fish known to be in the area could take up position on the shallower shelf under the abundance of cover to be found there.

Boat activity is always heavy on the Avon during the summer months, but at the start of the match it had not reached its peak and this meant that the opening hour was going to be very significant in determining the section winners. This meant that a good start was essential. It would be more difficult to make up any deficiencies around midday when river traffic would be at its height. The fact that I was more local to the stretch than the opposition really gave me no advantage as all the competitors were well versed with the methods used and had fished the water under similar match conditions for many years.

As decided, I was to start with a waggler set-up, loose-feeding casters and hempseed to a far-river position. My float took slightly in excess of three AAA shots, the bulk of which were placed at the base end, leaving a No 8 and No 10 down the line, as shown in Fig 6. My brand-new reel line was 2½lb bs and my hook size an 18 barbless type, tied to 1lb bottom.

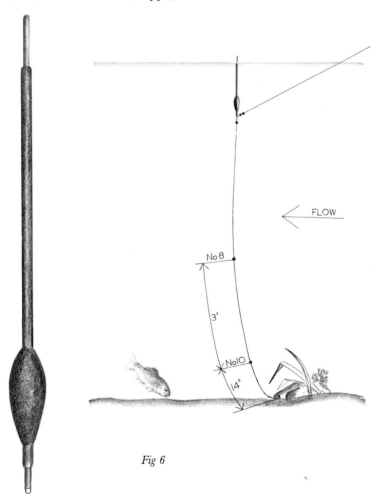

Fig 6

It is vitally important that a waggler line should support itself on the surface, even more so than with stick-float tackle, and this is the reason I used a new line. If it does tend to sink when a mending process takes place, then the tackle is so easily dragged off its intended course. A new line will minimise the risk of this happening.

Knowing the swim to be about four-feet deep, I set my tackle to drag about four or five inches, leaving a nice gap between the bulk shot so that the float could pivot freely when striking.

Eventually the whistle signalled the start of the match and I cast out to my far bank position, placing the rod in the rest positioned so that it left the butt very close at hand.

I fired some twenty or thirty casters with a few grains of hempseed to a point directly in front of me. In these early stages I was looking for surface disturbance because small fish intercepting the loose-fed samples can result in very little, if any, reaching the intended position on the river bed. If this is seen to be happening, then it is advisable to increase the feed to a generous pouch-full, say forty to fifty casters, on each firing. A little dodge I would also have used would have been to crush a fair amount of casters as a tempter to the small fish which eventually would follow them out of the swim.

I had experienced this problem in work-outs before match day, but for some unaccountable reason these small fish were not present in any troublesome quantity during the event.

I caught a couple of dace early on, samples of about two or three ounces, then my first chub followed soon afterwards, a fish of around six ounces. I was most interested in this species, and on the hour-mark I had some two pounds in my net and was taking a four- or five-ounce fish every few minutes.

I was loose-feeding the swim at each cast, but with the fish now established in the area, I cut the quantity slightly, hoping to maintain their interest for the duration of the session. I was quite happy catching these smaller chub because larger fish would undoubtedly have caused problems when they reached the pandock bed fronting the swim.

41

Fishing at a distance with the waggler float enabled me to tire the fish on their way back across the river, thus making them easy to handle close in.

The information from downstream was good as far as I was concerned. Both Robin and John, although catching odd fish at that stage, were beginning to fall behind.

After one hour—the period I considered to be so significant—I had about four pounds and had settled into a nice rhythm, still using the same hook, having no tangles and, at that stage, no broken catapults. All this did wonders for my confidence, and the information from my opponents' pegs was still very promising. I seemed to be leading the section quite comfortably.

As we entered the second part of this vital morning match something of a crisis developed when I was visited by, shall we say, a fellow angler, though my description of him at that time would not have been so complimentary.

He positioned his tackle just above my far-bank cover, and it was immediately obvious that his presence there was going to severely handicap my chances. I had no alternative but to seek his assistance and ask him not to fish until the morning match was over.

At first I thought he was not going to co-operate as he made a couple of tentative casts into the water. But these were greeted with a chorus of complaining voices from the crowd of spectators behind me, trying to persuade him not to fish. After this, fortunately for me, he thought better of it and rested his rods until the end of the match, preferring to sit and watch the remainder of the action.

But simply because of his presence there I had to make a tactical switch and shorten my line of approach. This brought me to mid-river and, although the results were not as good as those in the first hour, I continued to take odd fish until the end of the match.

As I had expected, boat traffic increased appreciably but this seemed to affect both Robin and John more than myself because they saw very little action during this latter period of the match.

At the end of the session the scales gave me a level 7lb and both Robin and John had scores of about 2lb. I was comfortably through to the big afternoon final, chasing that four-figure prize. For my morning victory I received £50.

My first thought then was to find out who the qualifiers were in the other five sections. This would be a good form pointer because I considered my bottom section to be about the worst among the morning matches.

As it turned out the outstanding qualifier was Nottingham star Pete Palmer who produced a catch of 13lb 8oz in 2½ hours. This was taken from the section directly below the stretch earmarked for the afternoon final, some 40 yards above the slipway.

The next-best section winner was John Illingworth, of Bradford, who was pegged immediately below Evesham Bridge and scaled 9lb 6oz, in the process edging out of the race my fishing colleague Ken Giles by some 2lb.

Leeds' Dave Thomas had the third-best qualifying weight of 9lb 2oz, and he was followed by myself, and then came Mark Downes, the Birmingham team man. He had occupied the peg immediately above me in the qualifying match and scaled 5lb 1oz. The man making up the final line-up was Phil Coles, of Leicester, who won the National Championship title on the Bristol Avon, the youngest competitor ever to do so. His qualifying weight was 4lb 4¾oz and it was enough to remove his mentor and well-known match star Ivan Marks from the competition. They were fishing immediately above the bridge.

This, then, was the line-up for the afternoon final. I put away my tackle—no mean feat with hundreds of people milling around —and made my way to the draw. This was arranged on the basis of the section positions in the morning match, each winner following in sequence, starting at the upstream end.

This meant, of course, that I was to be the last to draw and, in fact, my peg was going to be the one left in the hat.

The actual stretch being used for the final was from the famous white post (Peg 1) to a position some sixty yards above the slipway (Peg 6).

In my book the best peg to draw was No 2 with Nos 1 and 3 following. I didn't want the bottom swim, No 6, though in its favour was the fact that from some twenty yards below Pete Palmer had produced the morning top weight.

It was Pete, in fact, who was first to draw and he pulled No 4, followed by Phil Coles with No 6. As I stood and watched the pegs being drawn I thought at least Peg 6 had gone, and Nos 1, 2 and 3 still remained.

Dave Thomas was third to draw and he drew No 3, so things were looking good for me with three competitors to make their choice, and two of the best pegs still remaining.

John Illingworth was next and he drew stake No 5 next to Pete Palmer. It was more encouraging than ever, the worst I could do was to be left with Peg 1—and this is exactly what happened with Mark Downes drawing the No 2 spot.

On the way to my peg I thought I would find out how the public interpreted the draw through the bookmaker. But I don't really know whether it gave me confidence or not when I observed from Ladbroke's betting board that the odds were in my favour for an outright victory. The figures were 6−4 against myself, 5−2 against Mark Downes, and 3−1 bar.

When I arrived at the stretch which had been prepared for the final I was amazed by the number of people who had already taken up positions behind the pegs. Those from the morning match had moved on to the new course with many new spectators who had turned up to witness the deciding 2½ hours. They were something like ten deep all down the match length.

Straightaway I noticed that, as in the morning match, I had a pandock bed immediately in front of my swim, again making close-in fishing very difficult. In fact, as it turned out, my peg in the morning match provided ideal practice for this main decider. The swim depth was the same, some four feet, and with a broken willow tree in the river on the far side, I was nicely placed for cover. Indeed, all the pegs, with the exception of the bottom one, had good bankside cover.

I had given Peg 2 the advantage because of its inside line as this was an ideal stick float position and gave Mark Downes two lines of attack, one with the waggler and one with the stick.

With everything being so similar to the earlier match I chose the same float, a 3AAA waggler, similarly shotted, and didn't bother to set up a stick float this time. The water was completely dead just over the pandocks anyway, and I thought that all the variation on line which might be needed could be achieved with the waggler.

When the match started I cast towards the far bank, firing casters and hempseed in front of me, and after five minutes contacted my first fish, a chub around the pound mark. But within seconds it made itself fast in a midstream snag, and we immediately parted company! Not a good start, but quite unavoidable because I didn't know the position of the snag. At least I was now aware of it, so with a new size 18 hook, re-cast out to my fishing line.

Feeding the swim with every cast I was soon into another chub, a smaller one, but at least it put something on to my score sheet. It was about ten ounces and I slid it to hand across the pandocks without the use of a net.

This was only a 2½-hour match and I took a gamble on getting myself into an early rhythm, dispensing with a landing net as a hindrance.

I was heartened by the sweetness with which this first fish came to hand and repeated the operation with the following three or four fish. I couldn't see any of my rivals and I was in a good mental state and beginning to enjoy things.

First hiccup came when the resident passenger-carrying steamer approached the match course and I left my tackle in its far bank position until the very last seconds. With the craft only yards away, I had a bite. I hoped it was a small fish, facilitating a quick retrieve. But in the event I was left latched on to a pound-plus chub, and I certainly could not get it out of the way of the boat.

With only three to four feet of water, and the quite large craft bearing down on top of the swim, I quickly plunged my rod under the surface and hoped for the best! The last thing I wanted in a short match of this nature was to be chopped off some fifteen yards up the line, and with a good fish on the hook. I certainly didn't want to start re-tackling.

It seemed to take minutes for the boat to pass over my line and there was nothing I could do to discover whether or not I was still in contact with the chub. Tightening up would only have made a breakage that much more likely.

Eventually the boat had passed through and I took a deep breath as I increased the tension on my terminal tackle. I can't explain the relief when, with my eyes glued to the rod tip, I noticed the rod start to arc—the fish was still there! At that moment I felt about ten-feet tall.

I landed the fish successfully and looked upon it as a bonus in the net. After that, I could have suffered the loss of two or three fish before my confidence would have been affected. But this was not to happen. I enjoyed a good spell and caught numbers of fish right through to the late stages of the match.

Still not aware of how my fellow competitors were faring, I put everything into the last few minutes and it paid off as I hooked another reasonable size chub in the dying seconds.

Consciously, this brought my first decision on how to land a fish since I slid that initial chub to hand over two hours earlier. The whistle had gone and the fish was approaching the pandock bed. Should I use the landing net for the first time or should I slide it over the offending leaves into hand as I had done so successfully throughout the match?

Looking back, it would of course have been far safer to use the net. But there are few occasions I can remember when I have enjoyed such a good rhythm, and it seemed no problem at all in following the pattern I had adopted all through.

With the fish safely in the net, and the match over, all I had to do then was to await the scales to determine the 1978 Ladbroke Champion but, as with the draw, I was going to be the last to weigh in, as they started this time at the downstream end.

From bankside rumours, John Illingworth was tipped as the

likely winner, and for the very first time in the final I felt a bit insecure. Even my fishing pal, Ken Giles, was unable to furnish me with any information which was to give me confidence.

The only thing I could do was to assess my own catch which I put at about ten pounds, and then tick off the others as they used the scales.

Phil Coles weighed in first at 3lb 13½oz, but after all this was from Peg 6, the swim I didn't rate very highly. Then came one of my main dangers, John Illingworth, and I must admit to feeling very relieved on hearing his score of 7lb 13½oz announced. I was quite confident that I had the measure of that.

Pete Palmer, convincing winner of the morning qualifiers, returned a catch of 5lb 9oz, and next came Dave Thomas, such a prominent angler on this Evesham match length, and I heaved another sigh of relief as he put his 6lb 15oz on the scales. It was nice to have him out of the way.

We were now at Peg 2, the one which I considered to be the plum draw. I knew Mark had got off to a good start, having spoken to spectators positioned at the downstream end of my peg. But it had given me heart to notice a swimfeeder being put out from Mark's peg in the later stages. Surely he must have 'dried up' to have switched to this approach. But still I didn't know whether the method had brought him fish, or not.

I wasn't left long in doubt. Mark returned a weight of 7lb 10½oz, and I didn't need the scales to tell me that it was my match.

The officials eventually made their way through the large crowd to my peg. It was nice to be confident again, even without putting my fish into the basket, and the needle settling on 10lb 7oz put the seal on it.

I was to be Ladbroke Champion for the next twelve months with a four-figure pay-out and virtually an automatic invitation to the next year's line-up. It was a superb ending to a highly successful day.

By 1981 the format of this Ladbroke classic had been slightly changed to make it a straightforward 'one off' contest between an invited list of twenty-two of the country's top anglers, and fished over five hours.

With a field of such exceptional strength I was naturally looking for a little help from the draw in my bid to gain this top angling honour for a second time. As I saw it, possibly half of the twenty-two pegs could produce a winning weight, though with even two or three of these it was debatable.

The obvious place to be was around Isbourne mouth, a notable downstream area where for several weeks large shoals of chub had been resident and they had decided the destiny of several open events. Another fine area was just below the culvert which contained a multitude of small fish, sufficient to expect them to feed for the full duration of the match. Add to this the possibility of one or two better-quality fish taking the bait, and it seemed a place where the championship could be won.

The culvert itself had always been capable of producing a top bag, and this year was no exception. In fact the chances of this particular peg were probably better than at any time since the match was first conceived. This could be said, too, of the two or three swims above the culvert where again there was an abundance of small fish along with some better samples.

Then there was the bridge peg—the swim immediately above Jubilee Bridge. This had bounced back to form only two days earlier in producing the top catch in the Courage Championships at the hands of Mansfield star Colin Perry, and the competitor here would certainly be in with a chance of victory.

With all the competitors in this small but select Ladbroke field being given extra-generous swims, these pegs immediately above the bridge holding the better-class fish must be fancied if they were drawn by the right anglers.

I didn't particularly fancy the next six or seven pegs upstream, through the deeper water, but the top numbers, one, two and three, previous event winners, could certainly not be ruled out, though their recent form hadn't been all that impressive.

However, for all this conjecture, it was the draw which was to decide our fate, and when the time came for this I think everyone

A large crowd watching the author on his way to the second victory in the Ladbroke, Evesham 1981

was hoping to pick out a peg around the Isbourne area.

My close friend and England-squad colleague, Max Winters, was the fortunate one in drawing the plum Isbourne swim; and Dave Thomas, another 1981 international also drew in a favourable area, five pegs below the bridge, a piece of water which would suit his all-action style to perfection.

Former England team man Ken Giles was also fortunate, as he drew the culvert peg. The swim immediately below this was omitted, and this presented an excellent chance of the culvert swim producing a prizewinning catch.

With these attractive pegs all accounted for, I was still waiting my turn to draw and not feeling too happy about my chances. And when I did choose Peg 12, it was at first a disappointing number because, in the normal run of contests, this places the angler in a pretty impossible position in the deeper water above Evesham bridge. And at first I thought that this is where I would be fishing.

But I hadn't accounted for the double-distance pegging, and in the event I was sited at the bridge peg which only forty-eight hours earlier had produced the top Courage Championship catch of 12lb 2oz. But on viewing the swim, and assessing it realistically, I felt that even accounting for this previous success, it would be a hard berth from which to win.

We were going to be faced with intense boat traffic on this August Bank Holiday Monday, and being a shallow swim it would be considerably affected by the unnatural colouring-up of the water, to a far greater extent in fact than some of the other favoured areas such as Isbourne mouth.

In fact it was this big question mark hanging over the peg which prevented me from backing myself with the bookmaker. But I was still very enthusiastic and eager to get on with the match.

Having been at the Evesham venue for the previous two days competing in other Festival events, I had already made up my mind that if I did draw a peg in this bridge area then it would have to be an all-maggot job. I had with me a gallon of top-class bait, and being aware of the presence of lots of small fish in the area, I was fully prepared to use a big proportion of this ample supply.

My intention was to waggler fish at most points of the swim from a third of the way out, casting to a far line. In view of the bright, warm weather, I could well imagine the fish accepting the bait in a mid-water position.

I planned that if no visible bite indication via the float was forthcoming, I would briskly withdraw the terminal tackle from the distant line to a mid-river position in the hope of 'accidentally' hooking a fish or two as they mouthed the bait, an action which was not registering on the float.

This is, in fact, exactly how the match went, especially for the opening two hours. A number of these 'free' fish found their way into my keepnet and after a while the removal of some of these lesser-size chub and dace left the way clear for the better-quality fish to have a chance of accepting the bait.

The second period of the match saw me casting my 2AAA waggler float to a shorter, deeper line, and using the shade of the spectator-thronged bridge to trick several better fish into accepting my large single bronze maggot, impaled on a size 20 hook to 1lb length.

Two or three bream in the 1lb to 1½lb class also showed up, rather surprising samples for this venue, and sport didn't slacken for the whole of the match. In fact, though I had fed a near-margin line at the onset of the match with a few casters as insurance, it later became apparent that I would not have to revert to this nearer position.

As the end of the contest approached, large crowds both behind me and along the bridge watched as I fed a steady procession of small dace, roach and chub, with a few better-quality fish, into my net. Then, with five minutes to go, a chub over the pound mark accepted the bait immediately it entered the water, enabling me to finish the match on a high note.

As the final whistle sounded I remember reflecting upon one bream which I lost at the lip of the landing net, and a brace of chub which were obviously going the other way when I made the strike and which snapped my hook length.

News quickly got round that the men I had to fear, as I had thought, were Max Winters on the Isbourne peg, and Dave Thomas, below the bridge. They were reported to have catches into double figures.

I assessed my bag at around 14lb, and waited eagerly for confirmation of the other scores. News of Max Winters came first, he had weighed in 11lb 14oz, and I knew I had the measure of this. Then it seemed ages before Dave Thomas's figures filtered through—he had scaled 12lb.

I was now feeling very confident that this would not stop me from securing my second Ladbroke title. And so it proved. When the scales, registering a maximum load of 14lb, arrived at my peg it was with immense relief that I saw the needle spin round to the far limit, and lock itself there.

As I removed two or three fish from the pan, I knew that the

£1,000 crown was again mine. When my weight of 15lb 5oz was eventually announced it was quite obvious by the cheers that went up that quite a lot of lucky punters had backed me down to odds of 3−1.

That victory gave me a tremendous feeling. I had become the first man to achieve a glittering Ladbroke double.

4

The Courage Championships

In 1978 a new contest emerged which was immediately to assume the status of one of our most prestigious events. It was the brewery-sponsored Courage Championships which, through its unique format, gained a glowing response from match anglers all over the country.

It was on the lines of the other classic invitation events, and also housed on the Warwickshire Avon at Evesham, the Wembley of the matchfishing world. But the organisers had the vision to bring into the framework of the competition an opportunity for any match angler to win this fine trophy and glittering prize money.

To achieve this, they announced an invited list of top stars who would compete for the title, and in addition arranged a series of open qualifying matches through which other anglers could gain entry to the Avon showpiece.

There were no qualifications needed to fish these matches. In fact any angler could enter, all were treated the same, and tickets were issued on a first-come-first-served basis for the four scheduled rounds. Those lucky enough, or good enough, to finish in the first three in each match went through to the star-studded final, usually held on the August Bank Holiday week-end.

With such an opportunity, it was obvious that there was a heavy demand for tickets, and the organisers have always dealt with this situation most fairly.

The selection of the invited list of top matchmen was left to the discretion of the managing body. Of course, at times odd anglers with impressive records are left out as it is very difficult to arrive at anything like a foolproof situation. Certain areas of the country believe that their resident anglers should be automatic

Clive Smith with the Warwickshire Avon catch which gained him the Courage Championship title in 1980 (*Angler's Mail*)

choices, doubting the credentials of those elsewhere, and so on. But having taken all this into account, the eventual Courage champion is able to claim that he has beaten the very best in the country.

The overall field is a predetermined figure, usually approximately forty, made up of the twelve from the open qualifiers, four competitors from the organising club, one nominated by the brewery, and another two or three selected via a competition arranged by the sponsors, plus of course the invited list of about twenty.

The match course is usually from the white post where No 1 peg is normally sited, downstream for forty pegs, fairly evenly split above and below the bridge to finish just below the River Isbourne.

The event has developed a knack of producing very close weights and coupled with this no angler is ever very sure which swim will come up with the winner. In the first three years of the contest none of the champions opened up a gap of more than a pound, and the minor placings were equally as closely decided.

This was very much the case in the second year of the Courage event, in 1979, when I drew peg No 5, a swim with a nice inside stick float line, but lacking in far bank cover, which ended at the downstream boundary of Peg 4. Two pegs upstream at No 3 was Ken Giles, and above him, at No 2, was Ivan Marks. Both these pegs, in my opinion, are capable of producing an outright winning catch but because of their popularity they do get very heavily fished during the build-up to this type of match.

From my position I could see Ken Giles but had very little view of Ivan Marks. However, this would be a good yardstick to apply in my quest for honours.

I decided to fish two lines, one some three yards from the far bank, and the other down the near margin, about 1½ rod lengths out. I would use a waggler for the distant swim, and a stick float close in. But I had a strong leaning towards the stick float, probably supported by the lack of cover on the far side.

I planned to fish the caster and this would mean that for at least the opening half-hour I would not be making much headway in terms of weight in the net. But this was not to be the policy of the competitor on my downstream flank, Brian Jarvis, who was going to make his play with the swimfeeder, a method with which he had built himself quite a reputation on the Evesham waters.

Unlike the stick or waggler floats, the feeder tends to produce far quicker results in the production of fish. But this can confuse aspiring match anglers who have probably worked out with some thought that rather than forfeit the early period of a match by using a float why not kick off with a feeder and reap any benefits this may bring, then switch to the float at a later stage.

I have tried these tactics myself over many years but experience has taught me that in practice it simply does not work. Firstly, the expertise and mental application required successfully to feed a swim in preparation for a winning assault with a float cannot be acquired at the same time as fishing with a feeder.

The repetitive splashing of the feeder rig tends to wear down the swim after a while, similarly to the retrieving of this bulky tackle item across the water, especially on nearside swims when it is inevitably bouncing the surface.

Back to the match, and the scene was set. I was to work with a stick float, Ken Giles at No 3 peg would be using a waggler and taking advantage of the abundance of far bank cover, and my downstream opponent, Brian Jarvis, would be making his challenge with the feeder.

As I have previously hinted, at the onset of a match, especially one of importance in which the pressures tend to be that much greater, it is advisable to create a picture in the mind of what is likely to happen. I find that this gives protection against any hasty decisions which might be inadvisably taken in the heat of the moment.

The picture I formed was that Brian Jarvis would catch one or two better fish in the early stages of the match, but his peg would die off later on. Ken Giles would catch fish by virtue of the fact that he was fishing farther away from the near bank than I was, with a waggler, thus avoiding inside-swim disturbance through spectator movement, and if he could keep a flow of fish taking the bait, then eventually he could stake a claim to the title.

My task, with the inferior peg drawn, would be to try and build the basis of a weight using a stick float for the majority of the time, and hoping that because of it being less attractive, practising anglers earlier in the week had given the peg a miss occasionally, thus resting the swim.

On the start of the match, all the competitors in my immediate area used a far bank line. On my downstream flank Brian Jarvis's feeder landed just short of a weedbed across the river, and maybe the customary splash it created was further reason why I opted for the close-in approach.

Ken Giles was putting out his waggler with customary accuracy, together with ample feed, which is his practice when seeking chub, the quarry which we were all hoping to catch.

I set about the task of preparing a perfect stick float set-up, something I am prepared to take anything up to an hour to achieve. I found about eight-feet depth of water along the 1½-rod-length line, and shotted the float as shown in Fig 7. I was using a size 18 hook to 1lb, barbless, and my reel line was a new 1½lb bs strength.

My 14ft carbon rod gave me wonderful control in the slight downstream wind. The current was gentle, so that the light shots at the terminal end were important if I was to obtain anything like an overdepth situation. This is essential when stick-float fishing because with a fish facing its orthodox position, upstream, it is far more desirable for the caster or maggot to arrive in front of it without a column of line standing out, vertically, right in its sight (see Figs 8a and 8b).

I was feeding the swim with some ten to twelve casters each cast, but as the float was travelling the length of the run down I would flick in an odd two or three baits in order to offset any appearance of a regimental approach. At the start I had introduced a few grains of hempseed, say a couple of handfuls, into

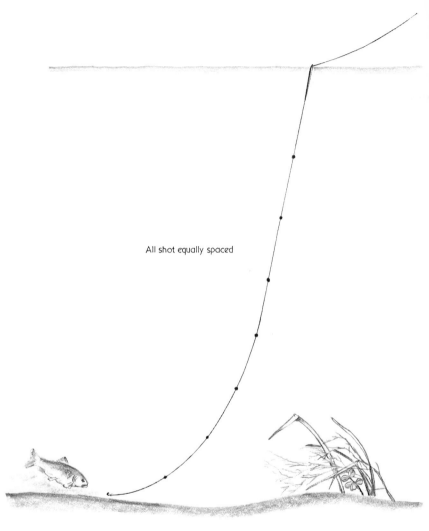

All shot equally spaced

Fig 7

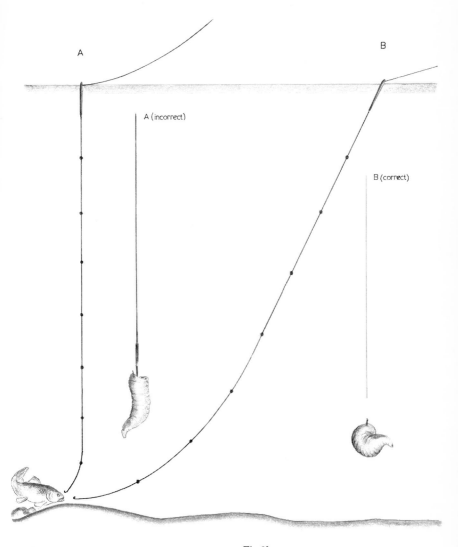

A

A (incorrect)

B

B (correct)

Fig 8a   *Fig 8b*

the swim some four or five yards downstream from me on my stick-float path. I also had another two handfuls in my pouch, making the ratio of caster to hempseed about equal.

To save time in this slowish water I was casting to a five-past position, and running over an area of some two yards. Brian Jarvis was two to three yards below the point where I was retrieving my tackle. As I have stated, it is not practicable to use a feeder then successfully switch to a float because of the disturbance created, and that applied to me as my float rig neared Brian's feeder-fishing position.

But it wasn't long before Brian was in action; following only his second or third cast I noticed a large swirl as he netted a 1¼lb chub. I wasn't too bothered at this juncture as this followed the picture I had formed, and I had not even had a bite. He followed quickly with another chub from his next cast, a fish of about the same proportions. I was still without a bite.

After only a short time a third fish was impaled on Brian's hook—less than fifteen minutes had gone and he had nearly four pounds in his net! I hadn't bargained for all this to happen quite so quickly, and his pace did not slacken when I had my first bite —a gudgeon. On the half-hour mark he had netted five chub, all about the same size. At that point the bookmakers had marked him down to 5–2 against favourite and I needed to draw on all my experience as the crowd of spectators he had drawn stretched to a point half-way up my swim. In a disciplined manner I had to ask myself, would he maintain this catch rate or, as I had pictured, would his swim eventually die?

I must admit that because of Brian's exceptional start, I made a reassessment of my position. I decided that I would give him eight fish inside the hour, then I would have to take a chance and follow his tactics, thus lowering my sights for a possible high placing. It would be very difficult to pull back eight fish with the swimfeeder because presumably Brian would still be catching.

About that time I caught my second fish, a nice dace, and, although I was not making much impression weight-wise it made me feel better concerning the performance of my tackle and also suggested that there was some life in my swim.

But Brian was soon into another chub, and that figure of eight was getting closer. I was now really hoping to catch a chub myself if only to suggest that I was making a meaningful approach. Then the screws were turned really hard when yet another chub, his seventh, finished up on Brian's hook. By then the crowd had grown tremendously, and it is not a very nice experience to have another competitor's spectators four or five deep behind your own peg.

However, just as he netted this fish, I had a good bite which set a fair arc in my rod. At last I had found a chub, although under normal circumstances a nice fish on the forty-five-minute mark would have been about right, or even a little premature. I played the fish gently, as I didn't want any other pressures at this time through a lost fish. When I netted it I was pleased to note that if anything it was slightly larger than the ones Brian was catching.

At least this success reduced his lead, and within minutes I was playing another good fish, a twin of the first. This was netted with the same caution. My immediate opponent had not added to his score, so this would put me some five pounds in arrears. But I was then beginning to feel a lot better about the prospects—even a few heads among the crowd behind me were now adopting an 'eyes front' position rather than angling their vision downstream to Brian.

I then started to catch fish at regular intervals, though not so big as my first two chub. I was getting a mixture of dace, odd roach, smallish chub and a few make-weight gudgeon.

Brian Jarvis seemed to have stopped altogether, and for the first time I permitted myself to look upstream in order to confirm that the action there was not too brisk.

After two hours and with six to seven pounds of fish in my net, there came a development which gave me a lot more confidence. My downstream neighbour wound in his feeder, and began to use a stick float. This made me feel good because to the best of my knowledge he had not prepared the inside line and of course all the disturbance created by the feeder would not help him. I was then within a couple of pounds of his weight—and still catching!

However, all good things come to an end. Just about on the three-hour mark my swim showed signs of slowing down, and, as if to rub salt into the wound, Brian Jarvis connected with a good chub, using his stick-float rig, which put him back in the driving seat.

At that point I decided to switch to my waggler-float rig, set up in similar fashion to that I had used to win the Ladbroke match some four pegs upstream. This time it was adjusted to fish at around the nine-feet mark with an extra No 6 shot added some three feet below the float.

The hook size was an 18, baited with a single caster. I had been preparing the swim throughout the match, anticipating a possible change of tactics, and it wasn't long before I caught a fish. My third bite produced a nice roach around the pound mark, and looking around I could see that the crowd around me was as large as anywhere along the match course. It all indicated that I wasn't doing too badly.

By constantly switching from waggler to stick float I kept catching the odd fish, and when the final whistle sounded I reckoned I had just about reached double figures.

The spectators intimated that it was the downstream section—more specifically the pegs below the culvert—which was most likely to produce the winner. Here, Pete Palmer, of Nottingham, and Gloucester star Tony Davies, fishing on his downstream flank, had caught fish for fish throughout the match.

News soon filtered through that Pete had managed to hold off Tony's challenge and was leading the match with a catch of 12lb 10oz. I feared that this was going to be a little too much for me, and when the scales arrived at Brian Jarvis's peg the position of the leader board was still the same. Brian was given a weight of 9lb 15¼oz and I think he will rue for ever the moment he switched from the swimfeeder. I think he would have been justified in expecting another four fish during the three hours which remained at that time.

When I removed my net from the water in order to weigh my fish I knew immediately that I was going to fall short of Pete Palmer's score. This was proved when I scaled 11lb 2oz and it meant that I was going to take third place.

Pegs 2 and 3, the favourites with such illustrious matchmen as Ken Giles and Ivan Marks, made no impression on the leading positions, undoubtedly owing to the fact that they had been so heavily punished during the previous couple of days.

I had enjoyed this match very much indeed but it was one which I wanted badly to win. With a third placing behind me, I was set up with a chance to do better in the following year.

I was fortunate in receiving an invitation to compete in the 1980 Courage event as early as May of that year. This meant that I could prepare myself mentally for this major classic, though of course all practical preparations at the waterside would not be undertaken until a few days before the match.

Over the years I have found that little importance can be attached to information gained about venues months prior to a contest. Methods seem to change drastically throughout a season. So much so, in fact, that if the angler divides his season into four-weekly periods he will find this a very useful guideline to cope with any changes which do take place.

For instance, the August period during which the Courage match is held usually brings a marked change in conditions. The very hot weather and accompanying low oxygen content of the water has usually passed, but we still haven't arrived at the period bringing the first frosts of autumn. In these conditions fishing can be at an absolute peak, and probably more predictable than at any other time during the season.

In 1980 the trend in most parts of the country was to saturate the swim with anything up to a gallon of bronze maggots and it was certainly producing exceptional results for a number of anglers. So much so that it was difficult to find many of them then fishing with alternative baits.

A couple of days before the match I visited the Evesham stretch in order to test a strong hunch that if I could make casters work as they had done in previous years, then there was a good chance that I would be very much in the minority using this bait. On studying the field of about forty competitors I was convinced that at the most there would be only in the region of eight competitors using casters. I was unable to accept that maggots were going to monopolise this Warwickshire Avon event.

My caster work-out formed an afternoon session at a peg about ten swims above the bridge which had already been fished by a fellow competitor during that same morning. My float was a stick variety, and I settled down to the task with eager interest.

After an hour I had little show for my efforts but of course this is not unusual when caster-fishing, if anything the maggot being far more instantly effective.

Just as a few doubts started to creep in the swim began to show signs of life, sport increased, and it wasn't long before I was into a steady rhythm catching nice chub at regular intervals. They were larger fish than I would have expected to take with maggot bait, and I finished with some ten to twelve pounds in little more than three hours.

I could have carried on fishing but there were a number of fellow competitors wandering about and I saw little point in putting on an exhibition. I returned home very confident that given a fairly good draw I could do well in the match.

When the big day arrived I set off for Evesham with three pints of casters, a pint or so of well-cooked hempseed, and six pints of bronze maggots—just in case of a disaster!

With forty or so anglers the draw is more lengthy than in some of the other classics, and I did not make too much effort to secure a place well up the queue. Eventually I arrived at the draw table with only five or six pegs remaining—but I was told that there were still a couple of good numbers among them.

One of these was No 2, a very high-rated Evesham swim, and I could hardly believe it when I opened my packet and saw this magic number. I had drawn very well indeed.

I shot off to the bookmaker to see how my odds stood. Before the draw I was offered at 20−1 and I had already backed myself for a £10 win. Now the rating had slumped to 6–1, and only minutes later they went down to 4–1 though not before I had another wager at the better price. From these figures it was obvious that it was not just me who fancied my chances in the match.

When I arrived at Peg 2 there was already a fair crowd of spectators gathered there. Upstream of me, at the top peg, No 1, was Barry Fulford, a very successful Birmingham angler and at that time reigning champion of the BAA Annual, the world's largest contest. At the peg below me, No 3, was Kenny Collings, the equally successful Southern star from Dorking.

Surrounded by such talent it was obvious that there were certainly not going to be any easy touches in the neighbouring swims.

On the far bank I had plenty of cover and there was a nice six-feet-deep run inside where I could use a stick float. The same applied to the No 3 peg; in fact they were very similar in all respects. But Barry Fulford at the top peg had the same bed of pandocks in front of him which had been there when I won the Ladbroke match. Now, however, the river was pulling a little harder after a week of showers, and this gave movement on the inside line. But it was dangerously close to the pandock bed into which any hooked fish would quickly run unless he was very lucky.

I planned to start with a stick float, though there was little to choose between this and the waggler. Perhaps the deciding factor was that Barry Fulford would be forced to fish well across with the waggler because of his inside-swim problems, and he would be the angler most affecting my peg because he had planned to fish the maggot and these tend to travel a fair distance down the swim before coming to rest.

There was little doubt that Ken Collings, too, would use maggots, but it appeared that he was going to start on the inside line also as just before the 'off' I noticed a stick-float rig nestling in his rod rest.

With my caster plan, I was fully prepared for the customary

slow start and expected to be headed in the early stages by both Barry and Ken.

It was Ken, in fact, who made the best start, catching dace and small chub extremely quickly after the whistle sounded, on his stick-float-and-maggot set-up. He was feeding the swim very heavily and after only half-an-hour must have had the best part of three pounds in his net.

Barry, upstream, was being troubled by very small fish which were taking his bait on the drop. This is a problem very common with waggler fishing and the accompanying slow fall through the water on this stretch of river. The answer would be to increase the feed until the small fish had devoured their fill and moved on.

I was at this point catching odd fish, mostly gudgeon with the occasional dace and one small chub. After thirty minutes I had at the most just over a pound, but with the tactics I was following this was well on course.

During the next half-hour Ken Collings continued to catch well, and my swim also began to respond, not with the same quantity but with fish of slightly better proportions, dace around the three-to-four ounce mark and odd chub to eight ounces. At the turn of the hour I latched on to a brace of better-quality fish, which was justification for the caster bait. I was then moving well, and along with smaller varieties I estimated that I had about eight to nine pounds in my net at the halfway stage. This probably gave me the edge among the pegs nearby, though I had no idea what was going on in the downstream sections.

This first half of the match had followed a fairly orthodox pattern with all three of us keeping to our original methods. Barry's tiny fish had now started to disappear, and he had collared a couple of better chub, though both Ken and myself were getting signs that sport was slowing down. When this happens the employment of an alternative method is a must if the peg is not to be killed off completely.

Ken was the first to make the switch, going out across the river with a waggler, and he started to catch odd fish again. The deterioration on the inside line at my peg had not been quite so severe, but although I was still catching fish now and again, after another twenty minutes I also decided that a change was justified, if only to rest the over-worked swim.

Ken was still using maggots, but I kept to the caster and went across river to join him with my waggler. I had been feeding this far line with casters from the start but the sport I was finding was not comparable with that of my neighbouring rival and because of this I felt that another decision had to be made, this time concerning a possible change of hookbait. The fact was, I was getting a very uneasy feeling that Ken Collings was closing the gap which I had opened up earlier.

After 3½ hours I estimated that I had about ten pounds in the net and put Kenny's catch at something approaching eight pounds. At the top swim Barry was still taking odd chub, and his score must have been four to five pounds. But then he took a chance in switching to the inside line, fishing some three to four feet beyond the pandocks with a 3BB stick float.

I scaled my hook size down from an 18 to a 20 and substituted my caster for a maggot. Immediately I started to take fish with this new approach. Also I introduced an occasional maggot or two into the swim as with only an hour or so to go, I was willing to try anything in an effort to catch those few remaining fish.

So I worked out a manoeuvre whereby after four or five unproductive swims down, underlining the negative response, I switched back to the inside line with my stick float and this brought an immediate reaction in the form of one or two fish. Here again sport was short-lived, in fact a repeat of my experience with the waggler. So I kept switching about between the inside and far swims, picking up fish from each area.

But in the dying stages of the match even this limited response petered out and with Kenny Collings, now fishing much shallower at about three feet, taking a nice brace of chub, I was anxiously awaiting the finishing whistle. When this sounded, in fact, he was playing another good fish but this one he eventually lost among river-bed growth.

Upstream, Barry Fulford also made rapid progress towards the end with his stick float and maggots. This left me with the thought that, although I had a reasonably good weight in my net, my neighbours were enjoying far more success in this late match period, thus suggesting that the bronze maggot had perhaps finally taken over at Evesham.

However, it was then all down to the scales to determine the result. It is common practice in these events for only one set to be used so that spectators can see all the catches weighed.

Reports that there had been some brisk action in the down-stream area were confirmed when Tom Manning, winner of the 1978 event, weighed in a good catch of 13lb 4oz. His upstream neighbour was nationally known Max Winters, of Gloucester, and these two had been matching their catches throughout. This was confirmed by the scales when Max fell just short of Tom Manning—by only two ounces, after a re-weigh.

At the upstream peg next to Max Winters was the in-form angler of the time, John Dean of Nottingham. Could he make the bronze maggot tame the Avon as he had done so often on his beloved Trent? On this day he couldn't, and he recorded a weight around the eight-pound mark. Two days later, however, he was to put his name on the Ladbroke Trophy with a weight of just under eighteen pounds at the same venue.

There were other good double-figure weights through the stretch, and as the weighing party approached my peg I honestly did not know whether I had sufficient or not. It was just like turning back the clock twelve months, though Southern star Dickie Carr did try very hard to pin me down in assessing my weight, and I must admit to saying that I would be within three to four ounces of the top catch.

From Peg 3, Ken Collings weighed in a high 11lb, and then it was my turn. After finding that the scales weighed a maximum of 14lb, and knowing how critically balanced the match was at that stage, I opted to have two separate weighings. I first put just over double figures into the tray, the needle settling at 10lb 5oz, which meant that I needed a second reading in excess of 2lb 14oz to give me this coveted title.

The outsize winner's cheque being presented to the author at the end of the 1980 Courage Championship

Looking at the remaining fish in my net I thought I could have just enough, but was this wishful thinking? Only the scales would tell.

I tipped the rest of my fish into the tray and it seemed ages before the scalesman hooked it on to the scale. The needle moved at last and it was immediately obvious that it was going to settle beyond the 3lb mark. Eventually it registered at 3lb 8oz, and I had won the Courage crown with a total of 13lb 13oz.

There was the usual big cheer from the crowd—obviously quite a number had been lucky enough to have chosen me for their bets. Others, I should imagine, kept fairly quiet.

The presentation followed straightaway and that was when I was confronted with the biggest 'fish' I have ever seen. It was some five feet long, and was the design chosen for my winner's cheque—species unknown. It told me that I was £650 better off for winning the match, and with side bets added, the day's work had earnt me well over £1,000.

It was very gratifying to become the 1980 Courage champion after getting so close in the previous year. It was a title I wanted to win very much and, added to my 1978 Ladbroke crown, it meant that I was the first angler to complete the double on this famous Warwickshire match course.

5

The *Sun*
Pro-Am Championships

The *Sun* Pro-Am Championship has gained recognition on the match circuit for two very good reasons. Firstly, it is unique in the world of angling with its format of coupling the country's top anglers with lesser-known enthusiasts, very similar to the successful pattern followed in golf. Secondly, being the idea and promotion of a national newspaper, its status has been elevated and the match given mass coverage to an unconverted readership.

The paper's angling editor, Stan Piecha, well-known in top matchfishing circles, selects a line-up from England's leading stars, who form the 'professional' section of the match. The anglers who partner them are determined through a competition for *Sun* readers.

As can be imagined, with an opportunity to fish alongside the cream of the country's match anglers, this competition attracts a terrific response, and anglers of varying degrees of skill eventually gain places in the championship.

The event was launched in 1978 and the first three championships were held at Coombe Abbey Lake, near Coventry, a noted bream water and venue for many classic events in recent years.

This is not an easy piece of water to fish, though it contains some fine specimens. The resident bream are well above average size with fish between four and five pounds quite commonplace. This is an added bonus for the 'amateur' contingent in being given a chance to fish for specimen species.

From my point of view Coombe Abbey had become an increasing challenge. Although I had gained second place there in the 1969 NFA Knockout, forerunner of the Embassy Challenge, it was generally a venue at which I had enjoyed only small success.

In fact, as the 1980 Pro-Am classic approached, I was really beginning to question whether I could ever again get near to a matchwinning performance at this venue.

For the two or three years leading up to the event my match calendar had included about three contests each season at Coombe and I was totally familiar with the depth, and I was also well-versed in the styles and tactics needed to win matches there.

Although reluctant to point to the draw as an excuse for failure, I did feel that this particular venue had not been too kind to me in this direction. All the same, a nagging doubt had crept into my mind whether, even if I did have a sufficiently good peg, I could come up with a winning catch using a style of angling for which I am not particularly noted. After all, in this particular promotion the selected stars included some of the best bream men in the country, such as the 1978 winner, Leicester's Ivan Marks, probably at the top of the tree when it comes to fishing for bream. In addition, the following year the title fell to another expert bream angler, Northern ace Kevin Ashurst, who also won the first NFA Knockout at the same water in 1968.

A week or two before the match, Stan Piecha telephoned me to give details of the man whom I would be partnering at Coombe. This information is always very sketchy, but it can give confidence if the person concerned comes from a 'breamy' part of the country. The chances of success can increase if teamed with a matchman from the Norfolk area, home of the famous Broads, or with one based towards the east coast near the Witham, Welland or Nene, all noted bream waters. However, the degree of expertise possessed by the man with whom you are partnered is still unknown.

As soon as the pairings are made, it is usual for the 'amateur' competitors to contact the stars with whom they are teamed in order to gain some information about the big day ahead. Their capabilities are quickly assessed in conversation and the 'professional' soon discovers what help he might expect in terms of weight secured by his partner on match day. But, of course, all degrees of expectation are accepted in the spirit of the competition, for after all the match does at least offer a day out for both the professionals and their partners.

For the 1980 match my partner came from Oxford, not an area particularly known for the style of fishing to be encountered at Coombe Abbey. We had a chat on the telephone when I briefed him about what to expect at the venue with an agreement that we would go into the finer tactical points of the match on the morning of the contest.

The match was being staked on the Linley bank at Coombe and from exploratory visits to the water I was well aware of the areas in which bream were most likely to be contacted. For instance, I knew that the most consistent stretch was that extending from the boathouse back for a distance of some fifteen pegs. A draw along this length would suit me fine.

On the morning of the match I eventually met my friend from Oxford, and his first important task was to make the draw for both of us. The joint draw was to ensure that he was positioned in one half of the course, and myself in the other. Under the system I would be fishing between two 'amateurs', and my partner would be pegged with a 'professional' on each flank.

I was fortunate in being given Peg 5, a swim located towards the boathouse, and one which I really fancied.

My team-mate was at the opposite end of the stretch in an area less productive than mine, so it was immediately obvious that if we were going to win it was up to me to produce something substantial.

The depth at Coombe Lake is around the four-feet mark, and this means that a very cautious approach must be made with groundbait. Although the water is slightly coloured, it is also advisable to fish at a fair distance from the bank because of the shallowness of the water.

I chose to work at about forty yards out, using 3lb bs line with a size 20 hook to 1½lb bs trace and a ¾oz bomb. Because of the expected size of fish I used a 5ft-long tail and a longish lead link around 10in because when righting themselves after accepting the bait fish of these proportions will easily lift a length of tail as suggested, and still register a bite on the indicator.

The type of indicator I prefer when fishing the Coombe Abbey water is a spring tip, though when seeking bream this is the only venue where I do select this particular catching aid. Of the many varying forms of bite indicator, such as the swing tip, quiver tip, spring tip, and even the float, on bream waters I have received no help from any statistical facts about each locality in making a selection.

For instance, I have enjoyed a reasonable degree of success at Earlswood Lakes in Warwickshire, a venue not far from my home, where the shallow-end section of the main lake is very similar in depth to Coombe Abbey. Yet there, I always employ a swing tip.

The only real difference between the two venues lies in the size of fish which they hold. At Earlswood, the average is little more than a pound while at Coombe it is nearer to four pounds. Perhaps over the years this has brought some bearing, subconsciously on the choice of tackle.

In most other styles of angling the final choice of float or swim-feeder can be made by consideration of instances encountered at other similar venues. But with bream fishing the most successful bite indicator is arrived at only by practical experience on the actual water in question. I have not found any short cuts in pre-determining this choice of indicator.

As the approach was going to be the same by all the 'professional' contingent, ie to fish exclusively for bream by legering at a distance, I suggested to my partner that we should assemble our tackle together, at my peg, following an identical set-up. This would give him confidence because it was going to be a match in which, because of the species being sought, there would be long delays between bites. To an inexperienced angler these long lulls bring on doubts as to whether his tackle will be capable of correct functioning when the fish do start feeding.

After making sure that my team mate had got his tackle correct and had all the proper bait, he went off to his peg, and from then on we were both on our own, as were all the rest of the line-up.

Coombe Abbey is an ideal venue for a 'stand up' legering approach. The water is very shallow in the near margins and I like to submerge my seat box and use it as a table top for my groundbait, catapults and other tackle items which are occasionally required during a match.

I set my rod on two rests so that the butt was near my right hand (see Fig 9a), positioning the indicator at an angle of 45° to the leger weight (see Fig 9b). Depending upon the wind, and in turn upon the waves created, I like to leave my spring tip as near to the surface as possible. If this isn't done any slight breeze on an unnecessarily long exposed section of line will create false bites all day long.

With all my tackle nearby I settled down in a comfortable fishing position ready for the starting signal. When it came it would be the signal for me to fire six balls of groundbait across to my forty-yard fishing mark. Because of the shallow nature of the swim these balls had to be as soft as possible.

This was another instance where there was no substitute for experience and any aspiring bream angler facing waters of this type would be well advised to arrange planned practice sessions for himself, equipped merely with a catapult and an ample supply of groundbait. It requires great confidence to fire a very soft ball of groundbait a considerable distance, especially in a match of this calibre where there would be numbers of spectators.

A fatal mistake, through inexperience, is for the angler to stiffen the groundbait in an effort to guarantee that it arrives over at the fishing area intact. All this does is ensure that the resident fish quickly vacate that particular area.

When fishing waters such as Coombe I use 100-per-cent-brown groundbait and work it into a mix slightly stiffer than I require it to be when it is actually fired. This is because in its stiffer state it is easier to force in more feed, such as casters and squatts, than it is when the groundbait is softer.

As with all other forms of groundbait, the live feed—in this case squatts—is added in such a way that there is little remaining

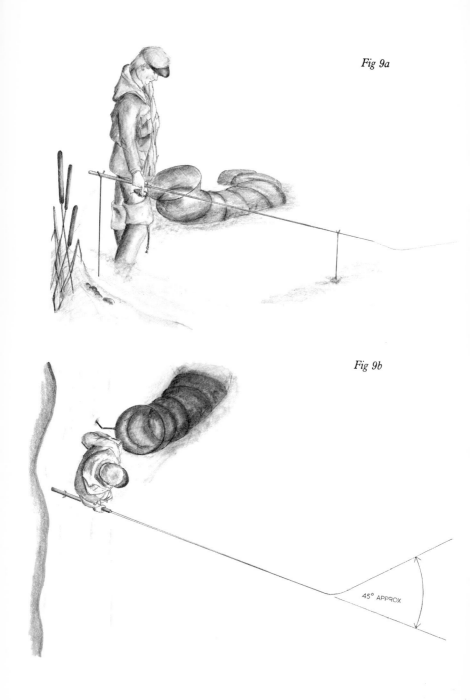

Fig 9a

Fig 9b

45° APPROX

surplus when that particular ball has been formed. The casters, of course, would have been introduced when the groundbait was first dampened.

The angler's next job must be to ensure that this ball, when entering the water, makes as little noise and disturbance as possible. As explained, the groundbait is made up of stiffer composition than that recommended for the depth of water, and as it is the perimeter of the ball which has the greatest bearing on the noise factor, this is now softened. There is a simple way of doing this, merely allow the ball of groundbait to rest in the hand and for two or three seconds submerge it in the water. If preferred a handily placed utensil can be used. This is called 'glazing', and the difference it makes in cutting down entry disturbance can only be fully appreciated by comparison between glazed and untreated groundbait balls.

But back to the match, and as it got under way I carefully lined up an easily recognisable far-bank position at which I fired four balls of groundbait at a distance of forty yards. On a large expanse of water it is most important to have a marker when feeding groundbait at a distance because if it is not carried out then the angler could find himself some ten or fifteen yards out, either with casting or his follow-on balls of groundbait (see Fig 10).

I intended using both casters and gozzers on the hook, and at times even one of each. But for the opening session I thought that two small hookbaits with the movement they generated could be more interesting than the static caster. I cast out to the baited area and settled down for what I knew could be a longish wait for any action with the style of fishing I had adopted.

When bream fishing it is vital that the angler does not excite himself because as long as his cast is accurate there is nothing to be gained by frequent removal of the tackle from the water. In fact, with a depth of three to four feet it would only have an unnerving effect on any fish in the locality.

At venues like Coombe Abbey, I think in terms of about four casts each hour when bites are not forthcoming.

The first ten minutes of the match went by without incident

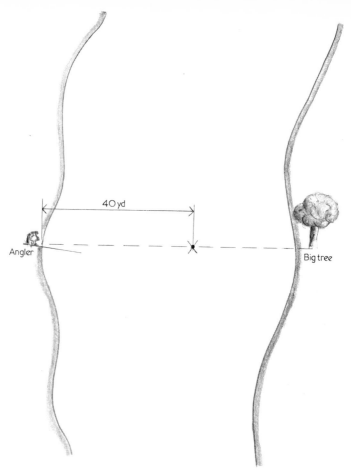

Fig 10

and, taking advantage of a strongish wind which created a fair wave on the water, I introduced another ball of groundbait. With the camouflage afforded by the blustery conditions, I decided on feeding a groundbait ball somewhere between the size of an egg and that of a tennis ball every ten minutes or so. In exceptional circumstances, of course, adjustments to this schedule would be made. This could be triggered off, for instance, by a complete lack of co-operation from the fish. After, say, three hours without any sign of action, then the benefit of feeding casters with the groundbait would be appreciated. It would enable the angler to slow down his feeding pattern, thus giving the fish a peaceful sanctuary and knowing full well that three hours of feeding will have deposited on the bed of the lake enough casters to arouse the interest of any passing shoal.

However, my first hint of action came after only half-an-hour in the form of a somewhat fastish pull on the spring tip. But it proved to be a passing fish which had fouled the line. Yet the indication was that of a bream, as a smaller fish would simply have plucked the indicator.

Then after another half-hour I had another similar indication on the spring tip, but this one of a slower nature. I was in no hurry to strike because early reaction of this kind with large bream often results in a complete lack of connection.

I would think that there was an interval of some four or five seconds between the initial movement of the indicator and my response, a slow but positive backward sweep of the rod.

I was soon made aware by the severe arching of the rod that a typical Coombe Abbey bream was fighting for its freedom at the end of my tackle some forty yards from the bank.

After hooking, it is desirable to remove a fish from the baited area as quickly as possible, and this is not difficult with Coombe bream because they seem to reserve most of their energy for resistance when they near the angler.

By movement of the rod rather than winding the reel, I applied constant pressure on the fish in what is best described as a 'pumping' action, taking up the surplus line on the forward positioning of the rod. In this way I gradually eased the fish towards a netting position.

In the later stages of playing a good fish in shallow water, it is advisable to position the rod as high as possible in order to prevent the bomb from fouling any obstruction on the retrieve. At Coombe Abbey Lake there are fairly large mussels which cluster and form perfect traps for an Arlesey bomb as it is dragged along the lake bed.

As the fish came closer I had also to be sure to keep it on a long line to counteract any possible lunge which it may decide to make. The easiest way to lose a fish just prior to netting is to keep the distance between the end of the rod and the fish as short as possible. In this situation, an about-turn by the fish will result in either the hook pulling free, or a complete breakage.

Eventually I was able to slide the bream on to its side and over the waiting landing net before carefully removing the hook and harbouring the fish, a specimen of 3½–4lb, in my keepnet.

Before my next cast I cleaned the slime from the line and changed the hook. This is a habit I have developed at Coombe because I believe that the time lost in carrying it out is well spent in terms of security when considering the next fish to be hooked.

It was twenty minutes or so before my double gozzer bait was again accepted by another bream of similar proportions, and a third fish followed after another similar interval. But then came a spot of trouble as either the fish, or the bomb, fouled an obstruction on the way to the net. It was probably one of those mussels.

This was a situation I had experienced many times before in my years of match fishing. Immediately I slackened off, rested the rod, and calmly set about firing a ball of groundbait into the fishing area. I was in no hurry to resume the action, so I transferred a few more squatts into the smaller utensil which I had positioned on my creel.

Some two or three minutes had now passed since I put down the rod, and when I again lifted it from the rests it was a relief, though no great surprise, to find that the fish had freed itself from the obstacle, and I was now in a position to land it.

When first encountering this snag, the worst thing I could have done was to have applied heavy pressure. This would merely have wedged the tackle in the snag and made it impossible for the fish to pull the bomb free. As it was it acted just as I had thought it would, in turning about and heading back towards the centre of the lake.

This third bream finally went into my keepnet giving me a total up to that point of around double figures. I maintained the feed pattern at regular intervals, at times adding two or three yards to my cast. On occasions when I experienced a couple of line bites, indicating that the fish were lying somewhere between myself and the bomb, I would shorten the cast by a few yards hoping to pinpoint their position more accurately.

As the match progressed I caught several more bream and the bankside spectators indicated that I was doing as well as anybody in the line-up. Unfortunately, up to that point my partner had failed to catch, so every fish I could feed into my net would be doubly useful.

It transpired that the previous two event champions, Ivan Marks and Kevin Ashurst, were my closest challengers, and as both their 'amateur' partners had managed to catch fish I needed to open a gap of quite a few pounds if I was to make certain of victory.

With a matter of only seconds to go before the final whistle, my spring-tip indicator again moved slowly in the direction of mid-lake. My last fish was on the hook, and, realising the importance of its addition to my weight card, the distance it had to travel to my net seemed far greater than forty yards at that moment.

However, all went well. I played the fish into submission, and all I then had to do was to await the arrival of the scales with anticipation.

My partner had not been able to open his account so it all hinged upon whether my score alone would be good enough to hold off the combination weights of Ivan Marks and his partner, and Kevin Ashurst with his counterpart.

My catch was weighed, and it turned the scales to 39lb 10oz, which on the day seemed good enough to win the event individually.

The next significant catch to be weighed was that of Kevin Ashurst, and this was marked up at 23lb 4oz meaning that his partner needed 16lb 7oz to beat my total.

On Kevin's left flank was the 'amateur' partnering Ivan Marks, and his catch of 8lb seemed more than useful.

By the time the scales had moved along the bank to Ivan's peg a big crowd had assembled. Taking into account the weight

secured by his partner, the Leicester ace needed 31lb 11oz to give them the title.

It became a nail-biting situation as with Coombe's large fish giving substantial weights a number of scale readings were needed to assess the total. But when it was finally calculated he had failed by three pounds to make up the deficit and overhaul my lone weight.

The partner of Kevin Ashurst, pegged farther down the bank, although rumoured to have a number of fish in his net, returned a score of only 8lb and left the pairing in third place.

This was something of a special victory for me. Not only had I won the match single-handed, it was a personal breakthrough at an out-and-out bream venue. Also it underlined the feeling that West Midlands anglers could beat the more specialised bream men at their own game, given half a chance.

Looking back, though, it now seems that the doubts I had experienced were not all that deep-rooted because I did speculate through a substantial bet with Jim Wooding, the bookie, and financially this made it an exceptional day. Furthermore, a *Sun* trophy was the icing on the cake. My 'amateur' partner went home similarly rewarded.

The winning bag in the *Sun* Pro-Am Championships, Coombe Abbey lake, 1980 (*Sun*)

6

The National Championships

My first taste of team fishing at National Championship level came in September 1961 when I made my debut with the Redditch outfit. The match was fished on the Trent with head-quarters at Gunthorpe.

This was long before the present divisional structure was even thought of, and the Championships were confined to one much heralded event looked upon as the blue ribband of match fishing.

It was quite a big occasion for a twenty-year-old, my age at the time, and my memories of that day stand out clearly. Apart from an odd visit to Wembley, I had never before seen so many coaches assembled in one place. Car ownership was then very restricted —hence the main reason for the popularity of the coach. But probably more important was the fact that this match was treated with so much enthusiasm, and a theme of togetherness and a meeting of old friends crept through all the competing teams.

This particular match was won by Coventry, a group who must take credit for a lot of what has happened in team fishing since the war. It was their third National Championship victory, and they were led by that legendary figure, the late Billy Lane.

This event had an immediate impact on me and there is little doubt that it sowed the seed of an immense interest in and dedication towards achieving good team results in the years to come.

I stayed with Redditch for the next three or four years, during which time I secured a section win on the Gloucester Canal in 1963. Then I transferred to the Provincial Anglers, who were one of the more successful Midland teams of the time. It was with them in 1967 that I fished what can only be described as a disastrous National Championship along the newly opened Great Ouse Relief Channel. There were more dry nets than I care to remember.

In 1969 I made a major change in joining up with Birmingham, the largest association in the country. But despite their size, they had never sampled victory in this prime event despite having taken part ever since its inception.

That year the team comprised roughly 50 per cent regular Birmingham members, the remainder being made up of anglers from my own winter-league team, Cofton Hackett. This was no coincidence because this league side had achieved outstanding national success, something which was dearly sought after by Birmingham. The fact that I captained the Cofton side probably led to me being invited to skipper Birmingham as well, and I took over the post from the likeable Harry Bickerton.

This 1969 match was on the Trent, a river which was becoming something of a cornerstone in my National Championship involvement. The river had fished well below par throughout that year, its predominantly roach population being affected by UDN, the damaging fish disease.

Despite this, though, the midweek practices which we carried out produced reasonable results, and we looked forward to match day with a certain amount of enthusiasm. But then came an upsetting factor.

Heavy rain prior to the match pushed up the level of the river by some two feet, thus making it a difficult exercise for all the competing teams.

Under the weight system which was then still in operation we had a few mediocre scores, our best catch of 5lb 6oz coming from Lloyd Davies, and we scrambled into fifth place among the field of 114 teams. The individual winner, Roy Else of Lincoln, managed to record 9½lb, an indication of the very moderate sport on that particular day.

The National Championship team title went to Stoke, led by another equally legendary figure, Benny Ashurst, of Leigh, Lancs. But the day was not a total failure for us, as we did mount the rostrum to collect the NFA Bowl for our fifth placing.

It was an encouraging start to this new period with Birmingham and it certainly filled me with an incentive to steer the team to far greater future heights.

For the next year's Championship the side was strengthened by the inclusion of one or two young in-form matchmen, and under the managership of the late 'Mac' Holland, who over the years became such a father figure to Birmingham, team spirit took on a much more consolidated look.

But this 1970 event, on the Middle Level Drain, was a bream match, and as such was not going to favour us very much at all. Also, as very often happens on this type of water, one individual's big weight decided the destination of the team trophy. This was a catch of over thirty-five pounds landed by Brian Lakey and it took his Cambridge FPS team into first place.

Birmingham slipped down the list to a place just within the first twenty, and this was to be by far our worst position for a decade. It was a hiccup in our fight to reach the top, but the team took a realistic view of the match and in no way did we let it interfere with our future aims and ambitions.

In 1971 came the first real chance for Birmingham to win this coveted title since I joined up with them. The match was on our own River Severn and, with 116 teams taking part, it was to be the biggest National Championship event to date. In fact, this extensive line-up was never to be exceeded because the following year the event was destined to switch to divisional structure.

This was also to be the last National to be decided on a weight count. In 1972, along with the divisional system, points were introduced for the first time.

Birmingham AA assumed responsibility for organising the Severn event, and to this day I have not competed in a better-run contest. The headquarters was at Stourport, in the civic centre, then only recently opened.

That year, for the first time since I joined up with Birmingham, I was as near as I could be to being satisfied with the team. In fact, for the first time I was in the happy position of having thirteen anglers all worthy of a team place. It was Billy Stroud who was eventually slotted into the reserves and I was disappointed not to see him in the line-up.

However, I had a team tailor-built for the job, including classical Severn names such as Ron Russell and Stan Lewis. Added to this was the wonder boy of the early 70s, Lloyd Davies, plus established Birmingham names like Austin Clissett and Ken Giles. But perhaps the biggest ripple to go through the angling world for some time was caused by the inclusion of John Toulson, the Nottingham star, and Lancashire top man, Kevin Ashurst. In signing up these big names we had adopted a football style approach by gathering in talent irrespective of residence.

Although there were the critics of this policy, from Birmingham's point of view it was a reflection of our ruthless approach to securing top honours. Criticism bothered me not at all, and with ingredients such as this it was difficult to see how the team could fail to give a good account of itself.

We practised relentlessly right up to the match, covering every section from Grimley to Linley, a distance of some thirty miles.

Our confidence grew week by week, with 'Mac' Holland becoming more excited than the rest of the team put together. We had no slackers, and by match day the team men and reserves alike had all put us in a position of extreme optimism.

This 1971 National really captured people's imagination in the Midlands and I well remember on match eve finding it very difficult to prepare my tackle as I was called upon to make a television appearance, then attend a big function in Stourport itself.

However, the following day saw me up early and off to the venue for a pre-arranged meeting and final talk with the rest of the team. It was a lovely day, the river was in perfect trim, which meant that we should have no excuses for not giving a good performance.

Naughton Dunne, one of our enthusiastic reserves, was at the front of the draw queue saving my place, and as 8am approached I was ready to execute the only part of the proceedings for which we could not legislate, despite all our meticulous preparation.

That was the drawing of the peg which would decide the destiny of our team along the thirty-mile match course.

The bookmakers made Birmingham favourites at 5−2 against, with Leicester at 5−1, and few would argue with their judgment, certainly not myself. After studying the team positions in the respective sections, it was somewhat ironical when I boarded the coach that the man who should sit beside me was Ivan Marks, the Leicester skipper.

Leicester and Birmingham were ten pegs apart throughout the match length, which made it ideal for spectators who wanted to watch these two great teams do battle.

We were heading for Boreley, a section just upstream from Holt Fleet bridge and some five or six miles below the match headquarters at Stourport. It was hard to imagine either Ivan or myself as individual winners from here, but this was not important to either of us, nor to the remainder of our team members.

The Leicester captain was at the well-known bottom swim on the Boreley stretch used for open matches, while I was drawn on an unknown section of bank being used for the first time under match conditions. There was little to choose between the pegs as regards river characteristics, but I wasn't too happy to find that I was to fish from a landing stage. I always prefer standing in the water rather than being positioned some three or four feet above it, thus forcing me to adopt a sitting-down position.

The team tactics for my section were to employ a stick float some 1½-rod-lengths out from the bank, feeding hempseed and casters, and offering a caster on the hook. In fact, this was our policy for many of the central sections, but above Bewdley we were favouring the waggler float, here again feeding with hempseed and casters.

We considered the downstream sections, particularly the bottom two lengths, to be more favourable for bleak in gaining a respectable weight.

At my Boreley peg I was starting to put things together quite nicely when an inconsiderate boating club decided to hold a yacht race in the area—and this with hardly any wind! They certainly ruined the fishing for the last two hours of the match.

My final weight was 11lb 8¾oz, and it was enough to beat Ivan Marks by about 1lb. In that area it had been an exciting day for the spectators who had been constantly switching attention between our two pegs.

We boarded the coach together, no doubt wondering which one of us would take home the big trophy, but neither dared to mention the subject.

Back at headquarters it was the usual situation with the whole area rife with rumours. But it soon became clear that it was the two-horse race which had been predicted. My team had some excellent returns, and so had Leicester, though the individual top scorer on this day of big names was Robin Harris, MBE, Peterborough and England, ex-world champion, who scaled 40lb 5oz from a lower Quatford peg later to become known as 'Harris's Hole'.

Our new signing, John Toulson of Nottingham, had given us a wonderful start with more than thirty pounds from a peg opposite the bottom of the spinney at Hampton Loade, which he compiled using a waggler float. But from the same area Roy Marlow produced a very similar catch for Leicester from below the ferry. Ten pegs below John Toulson and also fishing for Leicester, Dave Rossi produced a catch of 20lb from a swim which was thought incapable of such a weight. The significance of this effort was to be realised more fully a little later.

As the rest of the weights trickled in, slowly we came to realise that our big bid for premier honours was likely to fail narrowly. Some three hours later the mammoth task of evaluating the match statistics was completed, and with thousands of people in the Civic Centre, and almost as many outside the building, listening through a relay system, the results were announced.

Following the normal practice, the individual winners were the first to be given and we were all very pleased to see John Toulson rewarded for his fine performance with third place. Robin Harris left the stage with the customary armful of trophies to a great ovation, and then it was time for the team results.

It seemed the usual eternity having to wait while the placings from tenth upwards were announced, but our worst fears were confirmed when Birmingham were asked to mount the rostrum to collect their second-place trophies and medals.

Our great rivals Leicester were worthy winners on the day, having put together 11lb more than ourselves with a total catch of 124lb 8oz 8dr, and their just reward was the coveted National Championship Trophy.

Looking back on that great performance, I firmly believe that it was Dave Rossi, fishing some two pegs above the pipe bridge at Hampton Loade and producing that 20lb from what was believed to be one of their poorer positions, who was responsible for denying Birmingham the trophy, and their first-ever win in the event.

All in all, Birmingham's performance was of a very high standard and, with the 1972 event in mind, was perhaps the best motivation we could possibly have had.

That Championship title still eluded us, but from then on we had the confidence to know that under the newly introduced points system we were going to take a lot of beating.

We had built up within the side a code of professionalism whereby these National Championship contests were a continuous project. We had done away with the system whereby a team is selected only some six weeks before the match, and then everything from transport arrangements to tactics is expected to happen in the short time remaining.

We were working twelve months at a time and having the help of the winter leagues, in which 80 per cent of our team fished under the Cofton Hackett banner. This was keeping us all match-fit for the large majority of the season.

The 1972 National was ideal for Birmingham inasmuch as it was tactically a similar event to that on the Severn in the previous year. The venue was the Bristol Avon, another water which would incorporate both the waggler and stick floats and obviously this would enable us to retain virtually the same team.

The only change we made was to bring in Billy Stroud, very

justifiably, to take the place of Jim Rider, who had been such a good team member for the previous couple of years, but who was now unavailable.

We kept to the same format which had so nearly brought us the title in 1971. We had developed a system of holding meetings in order to keep members familiar with one another and generally discuss tactics. The practical preparation had been condensed into the four weeks prior to match day. These were midweek work-outs in which all relevant methods and tactics could be tried outside the normal pressures of match conditions.

The task on the Bristol Avon was made much easier for us by it again being a venue which suited our style of fishing. In addition, it was a very pleasant part of the country to visit.

On the four Wednesdays prior to the match we had 100 per cent team turn-outs as our fifteen-strong squad hammered out ways of catching what we hoped would be more fish than any of our rivals. These practices were carried out in extremely fine weather, though this made fishing a little difficult with sport sluggish in the high temperatures.

It emerged from these work-outs that fish could be caught during the opening stages of any session by fishing the surface with a greased-line set-up. A size 20 hook to 1lb bottom and a maggot, with a 2in length of untreated cane as a casting weight (see Fig 11) was all that was needed to catch these surface feeders.

A 10–15ft pole was used in conjunction with this tackle set-up and it brought varying degrees of success, largely dependent upon the amount of cover available at the swim, which in turn determined how long these fish would feed before becoming suspicious.

For feed, a few maggots and crushed casters were thrown into the swim with each cast, and at the same time a far-bank waggler peg would also be cultivated.

On the Bristol Avon there are not many stretches where the far bank is not accessible, and with double-bank pegging something hardly ever encountered on the river the waggler was to become the base method throughout our team.

91

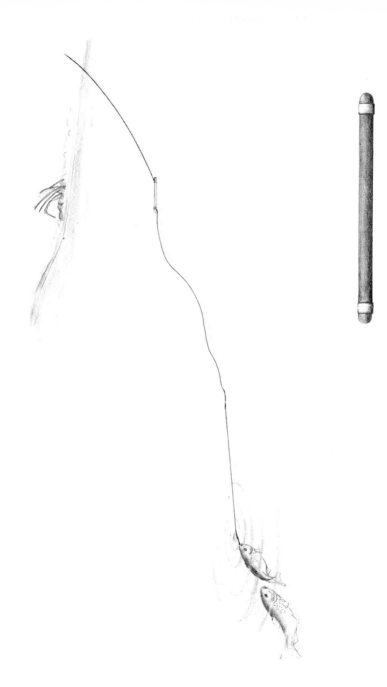

Fig 11

Because of the slowish nature of the river in many parts, the stick float at this time of year is less effective. But nevertheless, we thought that this could be a 'drop back' method to catch a few odd fish, at the same time serving to rest the waggler line.

This, then, was our team plan. All members were to commence fishing on the surface, at the same time feeding a far-bank line, knowing that the surface-feeding method served a double purpose in also baiting a stick-float line if required as a last resort.

It was a wet journey to RAF Colerne in Wiltshire on the morning of the match, and also heavy rain in the Mendip Hills had led to a cold-water influx into the river—with an accompanying drastic lowering of the water temperature—which put our carefully prepared plan in jeopardy.

We had a quick team meeting to discuss the big question mark hanging over what we thought was the ace up our sleeves—the surface-fishing method. It was decided still to set up the tackle for this approach, but to attack with a waggler or stick float straight from the start and look upon the surface method as an outside chance. Another adjustment to plans made at this hastily convened tactic talk stemmed from the view that with extra pace to the water the stick float would come more into the reckoning as a method likely to produce substantial results.

As we left for our pegs after the draw we were all hoping that the conditions would not deteriorate during the day to the extent that all our preparations would be wrecked.

Though I drew one of the best sections at Claverdon, I was unfortunately in a poor area. On my upstream flank was John McCarthy, a Southern matchman who had done very well in open events on the river leading up to the National. He was fishing for Calpac, the South's most fancied team.

I set up both a waggler and stick float with my pole rig, not knowing the area in which I was pegged and surprised to find the depth around fourteen feet. In my book this wasn't an ideal depth for a September match, so I was very glad to hook my first fish, a chub of about eight ounces, when fishing waggler style.

For the next couple of hours I caught odd chub, but when I sensed that the river was speeding up I switched to a heavy stick float and fished a more inside line.

I hooked one very good chub but unfortunately a branch of a tree travelling downstream fouled the line and caused me to lose the fish. This fish would have guaranteed a jump in my final points total.

In that first National to be decided over points *all* fish took on a new dimension, but at the weigh-in I was far from happy with my low catch just short of 3lb. I was on a section which was barred to spectators, so I had no idea how the river had fished generally, but my confidence was given a boost when I learned that John McCarthy above me had 'gone dry'.

Among the competitors on the coach, which normally hold about a third of each section, returning to headquarters, I was third best, which was quite pleasing, and when I got back to base and met the rest of my team the initial outlook was quite rosy.

It was difficult, under the new points system, for captains to assess their teams' performances. Looking back, it was quite laughable to hear of all the many section wins and high places which were being claimed and talked of. Well I remember that one northern outfit was convinced they had no fewer than five section winners, and another two or three of their members in the first three. In the event they finished about tenth!

Time wore on as the officials encountered calculating problems under the new system, and nervous tension gripped all those teams who considered themselves in with a chance of winning. Unlike in the weight system, it was difficult to arouse any confidence as to the final result.

But eventually the officials appeared, marching in column clutching clipboards, then mounted the rostrum one by one. A couple of blows down the microphone, a '1-2-3 testing', and we were ready to hear the 1972 results!

First came the individuals, and again John Toulson had performed miracles for us with a catch of 18lb and fourth place to follow his third position in the previous year. But the star of the

Clive Smith receives the National Championship trophy from NFA official Jack Musson following the Birmingham team's victory in the 1976 Division I championships on the River Trent

individual ceremony was undoubtedly the young member of the Leicester team—where have we heard that name before?—Phil Coles, who had put together a remarkable weight of 33½lb. He was the youngest-ever individual winner of the event.

Team placings were then announced, starting with the tenth, and we waited with increasing relief as Birmingham's name was not mentioned as the officials went through the list. When it came to second place the tension was unbearable.

It seemed as if the officials sensed the anxiety we all felt as they delayed the announcement for what to us seemed like minutes. Eventually it was revealed: Nottingham AA was second. They must have thought they were the most popular team in the country judging by the response they received, a substantial proportion of which came from our relieved Birmingham team.

To us the announcement of the winners now seemed a formality, but nevertheless it was met with relief as Birmingham were heralded as the 1972 champions. I know there were a few tears among the team at that moment, but the biggest ones were shed by our manager, who had lived every minute of the whole campaigning and had been connected with Birmingham for more Nationals than he would care to remember.

It was the third time in four years that I had mounted that rostrum on behalf of Birmingham, but there were no feelings to compare with those I felt at that first National Championship victory.

In recognition of that first National success by a Birmingham team we were given a civic reception at the Town Hall, and a sumptuous, no-expense-spared banquet by the Birmingham Anglers' Association.

The next year, in 1973, the match went back to a Fenland venue, the River Witham. We carried out exactly the same plan which had proved so successful in the previous two years, keeping the team together throughout the winter months and practising relentlessly at the venue in the few weeks prior to the match.

We set our stall to catch small fish, using waggler-float tactics, thus treating the points with the respect they deserved. Not for us the all-or-nothing bream tactics which could lead either to section winners or zero placings.

But our approach was too negative and led us into an early pitfall in those new points Nationals. The lesson we had to learn from that particuar match, in which we finished seventh among the eighty competing teams, was always to remain an attacking force. We had to be prepared to temper complete failure with a second method, but never switch to this alternative without first fully exploiting the potential of the original attack.

There was some criticism of the 1974 event, held on the Welland, because of the date chosen, 28 September. This was thought by many Welland experts to be some four weeks too late if the best was to be obtained from the river.

96

For Birmingham it was a doubly unfortunate date, for in their wisdom, or otherwise, the NFA had picked upon a time which clashed with the World Championships, which meant that we were to lose the services of three of our top members who were on international duty.

Again we followed our normal procedure in the build-up to the match and when the day arrived all the competing teams realised that it was going to be very hard going.

The river had settled into a clear state and fish were very hard to come by. In practice we found that first to get a fish into the net was a priority. It was in direct contradiction to the lesson we had learned in the previous year, but it was justified by the difficult conditions—cold and blustery, with gin-clear water. Dry nets were going to be commonplace.

Our plan was to start fishing very close into the side with a tiny size 26 hook baited with a squatt in order to try and catch a fish irrespective of size or species. There are numbers of small fry-type roach in the Welland, and if one of these could be encountered then guaranteed points would be forthcoming.

Well I remember placing my bowl in the water among the duckweed just before the match started in order to mix my groundbait and I noticed that one of these small fish was swimming about in the container when I placed it on the bank. The temptation was enormous!

However, when the whistle sent us on our way I set about legally catching my first fish and after only fifteen minutes was very relieved to feed a small roach of about two inches into my net. I was then free to attack the river for better-quality targets.

As far as I could ascertain one of these small fish would register the same score as three or four of them on the scale and there seemed little point in pursuing them. Also, they weren't easy to catch. So I cast to the far side of the river with a large float, and after an hour found myself playing a nice 4lb bream—on a size 20 hook! I was indeed glad to see this fish slide over the rim of the landing net, and during the following ninety minutes I had one further bite which produced an 8oz roach.

At that point I switched to a leger rig and this brought me another five bream, bringing my total catch to 20lb 6oz and giving me quite a high overall individual placing.

Birmingham went on to finish a creditable fifth, and Leicester recorded their second victory within four years, beating Coleshill by a single point.

The 1975 event was staged in the same area of the country, on the Nene, with six sections pegged along the natural river and six sections on the North Bank. Our practice for the match was confined to these six latter sections as we felt that any method determined for this stretch of water would be the fulcrum of our plans. Any team who could gain a respectable points tally here would take a lot of overhauling on the topsyturvy sections upstream.

Again we used the pattern of using the four weeks prior to the match to try and fashion an exclusive method for this North Bank.

Looking back, it is obvious that the vast amount of interest and activity created by the successful use of tares in the lead up to the match proved the undoing of very many teams. Against our normal policy we allowed ourselves the luxury of fishing the well-known Hospital Cup event a few days prior to the National, and our confidence was lifted considerably when we carried off the team trophy.

Our method for the North Bank was to ignore all seed baits as being unreliable, and to fish the waggler some three to four rod lengths out from the bank, using pinkies as feed with a small maggot on the hook (see Fig 12). We hoped that this would attract small roach, maybe bream, at all depths from mid-water to the river bed. Our target weight was three to four pounds per man, and we were confident of achieving this.

Our six team men on the North Bank included the three youngest members—Mark Downes, Paul Evans and Ted Farmer —and they knew, along with Tony Reece, Tony Scott and myself that the destiny of the First Division title lay in our hands. Birmingham were favourites to win, and the responsibility on the shoulders of these young anglers was immense.

My own match went very smoothly, catching numbers of small roach, when some ten or fifteen minutes from the end Newark team man Mac Willis, positioned upstream of me, started to catch very well using the method for which he was well-known, tare fishing. He was pulling out a fish with virtually every cast, having previously caught very little. Though we had decided to

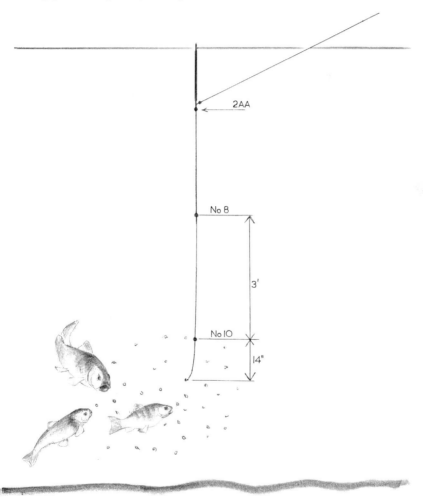

Fig 12

ignore tares as a team method, each member had planned to introduce them into the river on an inside line with the aim of preventing adjoining competitors from having any sole rights to any fish which may be interested in the bait in that area.

I could not help toying with the idea that, if Mac Willis was catching an eight- to ten-ounce fish with each cast, it might be well worth me trying to do the same. It was one of the hardest decisions I have ever had to make in opting to keep to my more negative approach. Yet in the time remaining I managed to add another five or six roach.

The outcome was very close between Mac and I and I went on to beat him by only 1oz, with a weight of 5lb 6oz, and collect a very useful seventy-eight points for my third section placing. Our other men on the North Bank had also done very well, and on arriving back at the coach I was so confident I told the lads that there was no great anxiety for us in that particular year as we were 'miles' in front. As far as I was concerned we were merely waiting for the formality of collecting the trophy!

Minutes before the presentation we made our way to the stadium. Sure enough, we were to record our second victory in this great event, but what a shock we had when we learned that it was by only a single point—from the little-fancied Rugby Federation outfit!

Shivers still creep down my spine when I think how near I came to putting a tare on the hook in those last vital minutes of the match. The ruse could have failed completely, and Mac Willis could well have beaten me, bringing an adjustment in points which would have been disastrous for my team.

I was proud of our young anglers that day and shared their delight when they captured a medal for the first time as actual fishing members of the team.

I rated that victory as a considerable achievement, coming from what was the stronghold of Leicester and other notable Fenland teams. But the water on which we were to defend our title in the following year was the Trent, now probably recognised as the elite of all the National venues. Here we were to take on the Nottingham team whose record was so impressive on their home waters, and equally dangerous outfits, such as Stockport, from the North, who had assembled a side bristling with Trent talent for this particular match. But we, too, had an exceptional team, probably the strongest Birmingham had ever had, and as reigning champions our confidence was sky high.

Our practice sessions resulted in numerous fish being caught on what is a very orthodox piece of water. There were to be very few mysteries about the 1976 venue; it was going to be just a question of expertise.

We planned to fish the waggler float on the majority of swims, incorporating a reasonable amount of brown groundbait, and using casters as the main bait. But of course the Trent is a very variable match course with large bends and changing paces of current. Some swims would be ideal for the stick float, and in those cases that method would be employed.

Once again when match day arrived we found that rain had affected the river. Competitors had hazardous journeys to the venue and there were many late arrivals. This did little for our peace of mind because one of our men, Paul Evans, was still missing when the coaches were being boarded. However, he did turn up eventually, and with a complete team we set about defending our title.

My peg was in the Holme Marsh section, and with our big rivals, Stockport, drawn next to us the five-hours' fishing ahead of us was going to be interesting indeed.

I wasn't very conversant with this stretch of water, but information had it that I had just missed drawing a potential winning swim, being three or four pegs too far upstream. Nevertheless I was told that there were fish there to be caught. Below me, Stockport team man Harry Jackson was pegged on what looked like an identical swim.

The pace of the river had already started to accelerate when fishing started, and I made my opening gambit with a stick float. On the half-hour mark I hooked and landed a chub of about a pound and hoped that this was the signal for others to follow.

But after another couple of gudgeon, and with a good hour of the match gone, I was struggling to attract bites. At the next peg Harry Jackson was in front of me and managing to take roach at odd intervals.

I persevered for another ninety minutes and, though adding a couple of roach, I reckoned that at this time I was a good three pounds behind my neighbour. The river was rising all the time and I needed a different approach to put me back in the race.

I took a chance on going across the river with a waggler float, a three-swan type, dragging the bait two to three feet on the river bed in a nasty downstream wind. I had previously been feeding a line some six to seven rod lengths out in anticipation of this possible desperation move. It took me a good twenty minutes to achieve the correct tackle set-up, and then what a relief when I caught a roach. It came just as I was beginning to doubt the wisdom of making such a bold approach on a fast-deteriorating river.

I persevered with this far line, adding a ball of heavy ground-bait at five-minute intervals and releasing the float to let it run down in the fairly fast water. The only slowing-down factor for the tackle was the line which was dragging along the bottom. For this, I allowed a good inch of peacock showing above the surface in order to prevent it being dragged completely under the water (see Fig 13).

As the match progressed my catch rate increased and I finished with just short of seven pounds of fish, not a big catch but one which pushed me considerably up the points chart.

I had managed to catch up with my rival at the next peg and beat him by about a pound. This was very satisfying for me because the Birmingham team had arrived at the conclusion that if we could beat the talented Stockport men it would probably remove the biggest obstacle to us notching up our second successive victory.

Back at headquarters it was very difficult to assess the position. We knew we were in with a chance but our team of 1976 was a calculating squad not given to over-excitement in assessing its

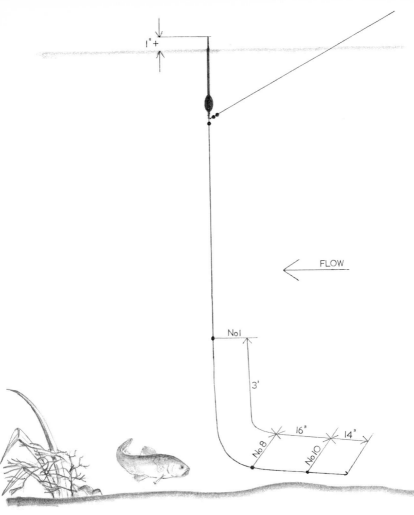

Fig 13

points total. However, I suppose this did give us an added margin of error.

We were reasonably sure that we had seen Stockport off. They had enjoyed little success against their Birmingham counterparts and seemed most unlikely to achieve a major placing. The main danger seemed to come from the Nottingham side, while Wyche Anglers, from the Crewe area, were the dark horses.

Eventually the calculations were completed, and for the first time in my experience of these presentations the team positions were announced in winning order. This confused me so much that when the acting BAA President, Fred Jennings, called Birmingham to the rostrum I wasn't sure which position we had gained.

Fred has not one of the most powerful voices and he had to repeat it twice before I was positive that we had, indeed, won this National, our third victory altogether and second in succession.

We then had a new target to aim for—a hat-trick of wins, something never previously accomplished in the history of the competition.

The 1977 season started with the Birmingham team committed to a very crowded schedule. It was the first year of the Captain Morgan knockout-trophy series, which Birmingham had entered somewhat reluctantly. If we had been aware of the types of draw we were to encounter we certainly would not have entered this new promotion.

We were drawn away to Oundle, away to Wyche Anglers, and away to Preston Izaak Walton. Coupled with the practice involved, this meant alarming amounts of time spent in pursuit of this trophy. Even more serious for us was the fact that while all this was going on there was very little time left to prepare for our National Championship hat-trick bid.

The match was on the Welland, for us a 250-mile round trip, and when match day arrived we had made a couple of visits to the main river, but had not even set eyes on the two sections on the Coronation Channel.

Our planned method was to start the match working with a pole and bloodworms just over the weed beds, at the same time feeding pinkies, similar to the tactics we adopted on the North Bank two years earlier.

There was some delay in getting competitors to the pegs because of doubling up of the coaches and I arrived at my swim little more than twenty minutes before the start. In fact, I was still assembling my gear when the match got under way, a

The Birmingham team-members celebrate in the company of Mr Bob Feetham, then editor of *Angling Times*, after their Division I success on the River Trent in 1976 (*Angling Times*)

situation far from desirable with an event of such importance. I find it very difficult to make impartial, calculated decisions for quite some time after having been rushed in this way.

However, I persevered with bloodworms and catching small roach, but I had an uneasy feeling that this was not sufficiently positive. At the next peg, Harry Settle from Leigh was catching better roach than me and he was fishing farther out from the bank with a waggler float. I was not certain of his bait, but suspected he was using pinkies.

After ninety minutes of deliberating, I finally made the change to pinkies—and started catching bigger fish. I made steady progress up to the end, but my rival at the next peg changed his approach to a swing tip, a method with which he had made quite a name in the North West. He caught first a big eel, then a nice bream, and at the end of the encounter there was nothing between us, as we each scaled 4lb 14½oz.

The weight was sufficient to give us a joint section placing of fifth with a handsome amount of points, and, on checking with the team members later, we all seemed to have done fairly well.

Our main danger teams, such as Leicester and Nottingham, plus Preston Izaak Walton, who were strongly tipped to win with their bloodworm tactics, seemed to be falling somewhat short of matching our team sheet.

When all the teams were back in the assembly area, a more detailed probe revealed Preston IW as the main danger. Their consistency with the worm bait had been very good, and it seemed to be a straight fight between them and ourselves.

That year there was another change in the announcement of the results. We were told that only the top three teams would be given. In third position were our neighbouring rivals, Coleshill. There were just two places to be announced—second and then first. Would it be a hat-trick for us?

You could hear a pin drop as the second-placed team was named—and it was Birmingham. It was just what we didn't want to hear, but from the Preston lads came a tremendous cheer as they looked forward to collecting the First Division trophy.

We filed from the stage, and the Preston team edged a little closer. But the following announcement stopped us all dead in our tracks. It was Coventry, the team of the 50s, who had pipped us all and produced one of the big shocks in National Championship history.

Preston IW had to settle for fourth place and my chance of leading Birmingham to that first-ever hat-trick of wins had gone for ever.

7
The Winter Leagues

The winter-league branch of match fishing originated in the heart of the industrial Midlands at Bilston, a dozen or so miles north-west of Birmingham, in the early 1950s.

In those days contests were few and far between, even during the popular months of the season. When winter came it was customary for many anglers to stow away their tackle and await more favourable conditions.

Wilf Hazeldine, the man behind the conception of winter leagues, reasoned that what was needed was a type of novelty event to encourage anglers to maintain their interest in match fishing throughout the hard months of the year. He formed a league in the Black Country area and it quickly caught the imagination of local anglers.

Now, to say that Wilf's idea has succeeded is a gross under-statement for there are now somewhere in the region of 800 to 1,000 teams, mostly comprised of twelve anglers each, taking part in league fixtures in all parts of England, Scotland, Ireland and Wales.

For many of these teams the ultimate goal is the *Angling Times* National Winter League Trophy which has gained increasing prestige over the years and is now generally recognised as being somewhat on a par with the NFA First Division National Championship.

A typical present-day league format involves about twelve competing teams, each of twelve anglers, taking part in six contests. The series can be calculated either on a points system, or simply by a weight count, the latter being preferred by the national organisers.

For the purpose of the National League promotion, the

country is divided into two halves, North and South, and the various league champions then fish against each other in their respective semi-finals, usually towards the end of February. From these two semis, the top three teams in each go through to a grand final, which in past years has been held both on home waters such as Coombe Abbey Lake and abroad, in Ireland and Denmark.

Up until the late 1970s this league structure was a little different in that it embraced twelve teams in the final, these having progressed from four regional semi-finals. This was when economic pressures were not quite so severe, and prior to that the system was even less complicated with a much smaller entry, all the league champions gaining automatic entry into the grand final.

It was in the early 1960s that Leicester started to emerge as a very forceful side and apparent heirs to the national angling throne, taking over from the super Coventry side who were fading after a tremendous run of success.

Although at that particular time they had failed to gain the National Championship title, Leicester had secured two victories in the Winter League final in consecutive years. It was their much-publicised quest to make it a hat-trick which fired me with a challenging desire to become involved in this league competition.

There were some very good match anglers in the West Midlands at that time but Birmingham had still failed in moulding a successful outfit, most of the members treating the sport purely as an individual exercise instead of knitting together as a smooth-running team.

At that time I was enjoying reasonable success and in the fortunate position of knowing personally many of the top Midland anglers. I started to approach them with a view to putting together what I hoped would be a successful league side.

It was fortunate that there was an established league in the area, the West Midlands Division, which at that time was dominated by the Colebrook club.

There was much enthusiasm among the match anglers I contacted and I received a lot of co-operation in forming what I believed to be an extremely strong outfit under the title of Cofton Hackett. The West Midlands Division proved an ideal schooling medium for us because Colebrook was highly respected; in fact many experienced observers classed them as well-nigh unbeatable.

On joining the league a big problem for us lay in the fact that it had been in existence for some five or six years, and the venues used for the series of matches were booked from year to year. This meant that not only was Colebrook a very strong team in its own right, but also was very experienced on the waters used for the programme.

However, we did get off to a wonderful start when we competed in the first contest on the Gloucester Canal at Pirton, a venue now little used on the match circuit. The event was run on the weight system as, indeed, all matches were in the mid-1960s, and employing an attacking style for roach we secured a first-round victory with a total of about seventeen pounds to leave the smart Colebrook squad trailing in second place some five pounds behind us.

This was an enormous boost to our confidence, and our success continued to such an extent that it was soon obvious that out of the twelve contending sides, the league had developed into a two-horse race. Each match saw Colebrook and Cofton in main contention, and there was rarely any other team able to split us.

We soon realised that the good start which we had made to the series had been very important because league points are extremely difficult to pull back when the same two teams claim the leading places match after match.

Our successful form was maintained however and we were delighted to finish as league champions at our first attempt. In those early days of the campaign it meant that we moved directly into the grand final with a chance to prevent Leicester from securing the hat-trick.

The venue for the final was on the River Erne at Bellturbot in

Southern Ireland where 144 anglers from twelve teams were pegged below the bridge in a downstream direction. The stretch was well known as a bream water in those days. I recollect that roach played little part in the match, their numbers being sparse compared with their abundance there today.

Leicester was a noted bream outfit, gaining innumerable successes on home waters such as the Witham, Welland and Nene, but this type of fishing was a little foreign to the Cofton team. We were given some leeway, however, with the final being arranged at the end of the English close season, thus enabling us to arrange practice sessions in order to improve technique. For those work-outs we chose the Twyning section of the Warwickshire Avon which we were led to believe was very similar to Bellturbot. The fact that we were then in the close season meant a little bending of the rules. Though legering was allowed, groundbait certainly was not, and neither were maggots. So, with this in mind, the whole Cofton team embarked upon some very-early-morning fishing expeditions!

We would leave home by 4am and be tackled up and fishing by the break of day, feeling fairly confident that the bailiffing force attached greater importance to sleep.

Practice sessions usually followed the pattern of mini-matches with our twelve members fishing in a line along the bank. The only exception was that we did tend to groundbait more heavily at the start because after a time bankside activity strongly tended to increase.

Well I remember one particular early-morning arrival at the waterside when heavy mist shrouded the whole area. We put our tackle together as usual and, on the given signal, our team of twelve let fly with the opening barrage of groundbait, using on average something like ten pounds per man. When the mist lifted some thirty-minutes later, much to our surprise we observed four all-night eel anglers on the opposite bank—seemingly in a severe state of shock as a result of our bombardment!

Those practice sessions proved to be every bit as useful as we had hoped, and it was a much-improved team of bream anglers which set off from Bristol Airport looking forward to its first big final.

We had a stormy flight across the Irish Sea, then there was a bit of a problem in collecting our bait supplies at Dublin, previously transported there by cargo flight. However, a treasury note solved this hiccup, and we were en route for Bellturbot, punctuating the journey with stops at local hostelries.

We arrived at the match area in the evening, and immediately made for the river bank to get our first look at the water. From the bridge we saw two or three anglers fishing some 300 yards downstream, and went to watch them perform. Within minutes we all realised that this was far from the type of bream fishing we had been practising. Our equipment consisted of 2-3lb lines, a few Arlesey bombs, and hooks ranging to no larger than size 14.

But it was apparent that these Irish bream of the mid-1960s had little knowledge of, and far less respect for, our English methods. They were wild fish!

We noticed that the local anglers were using hefty lines, about 6lb strength, and in buckets at their sides were 200-or-so worms of varying sizes, some quite hefty. It was noticeable, too, that their groundbait was very heavy indeed, and certainly nothing like that used on our waters back home.

It was quickly confirmed that this bold approach was the successful method as one of the anglers struck into a bream with a swift bending of the rod. Within two or three minutes he had the fish in his net—a specimen of about six pounds, black as coal and with eyes as big as 50p pieces! It seemed so substantial that a coat hanger could have been hung from the beading around its mouth, and the size 6 hook with the remains of a three-inch lob-worm did not look out of place. We were told that this was the third fish of that size caught by that angler in the space of thirty minutes! By that time we had seen enough. Luckily for us, shops stay open all hours in Ireland and within minutes we were buying 6lb lines for our reels and the necessary large-size hooks to replace our light gear. A few two-shilling pieces also brought us a few more hundred worms.

Then we felt that we were in a far better position for the following day's final, and in view of what we had seen we felt confident that any team who employed the English approach would fall by the wayside.

That night at a team meeting we came to the conclusion that three or four weights from the twelve anglers would produce the sort of returns we could expect on this type of water. Fish of this size do tend to shoal and, unlike smaller varieties, they are not resident at every peg.

Our plan was to chop up two- or three-hundred worms mixed in about twelve pounds of groundbait stiffened by pig meal obtained on the eve of the match.

We decided to throw ten balls of groundbait, each the size of an orange, into every one of our swims, and top up the supply at regular intervals. Because of the disturbance caused by this initial onslaught we did not expect to catch fish for the first two hours. We felt there was little point in pursuing negative tactics on the swims which did not have a 'breamy' appearance.

After a couple of hours the picture was indeed not too rosy and, as I recall, we had not a bream to our credit. It was a lengthy match course and our runner, Johnny Coles, was working flat-out to keep us all in touch.

After four hours of the five-hour match Johnny's report was still not one to become excited about. Although the odd angler along the match stretch had caught bream, we had none too many on our sheet, but all the team were sticking rigidly to the plan.

When the final whistle sounded my catch consisted of five big-mouthed perch which seemed to have tails growing out of the backs of their heads and no body! They tipped the beam at 1lb 4oz, and I made off with my tackle somewhat dejectedly towards the waiting trailer which was to take us back to our quarters. There was one vehicle for each section and it was some consolation for me to know that no bream at all had been caught in my section.

But the real surprise came when I arrived back at the marshalling area and one of our team men, Jim Rider, rushed up to me and asked what I thought of the results. When I told him I had not heard, he gave me the splendid news that Cofton had more than doubled the score of any other team! I really thought he was joking because, with only an hour of the match left, we had only two or three of our members with a single fish. It appeared that Lloyd Davies had caught five or six bream in the remaining hour, giving him a catch of something like thirty pounds and others of our team had also netted fish late in the match. We had, in fact, sunk the opposition without trace!

It was a wonderful victory because while all the other teams had failed to interpret the required tactics and had approached the match English-style we had re-thought our approach—the sign of a confident team.

On collecting the trophy and our medals at the presentation I had the distinct impression that nobody really took us seriously. The thought seemed to be that because we had fished so crudely, we had just been lucky: this made me even more determined to stamp our authority on this competition in the years ahead.

In the next season, 1966–7, Colebrook bounced back with a great performance in taking the National League crown on the Irish River Boyle. But we struck again in the following year to take the West Midlands League title and book ourselves a place in the final, this time on the River Rinn, a small Irish river reputed to hold large shoals of bream.

This was going to be a test in which the Cofton team hoped to remove those doubts which were levelled at us by the critics of our previous victory. We were still in the early days of match fishing in Ireland as far as English anglers were concerned, and with no facilities available for practice it meant that all the competing teams faced the match with very little inside information. Again it was going to be the side which adapted most successfully on the day which would carry off the spoils.

We had a full range of bream equipment, and having again carried out our training by means of close-season sorties on home waters, we were really match-fit.

Accepting that the river was of a small nature, it was suggested at our team meetings that a steady approach would have to be made compared with our tactics on the Erne, but still with bream in mind.

We were then a smooth-running combination and very much aware of the importance of our runner, Johnny Coles, who was still with us. In a situation where the teams had little information about the water it was vital to our success that John could obtain for us some tactical information early in the match to allow us, if necessary, to adapt our styles accordingly.

The Cofton plan was to make a steady approach for bream at all pegs for two hours, then reassess the situation with a view possibly to increasing our feed, or perhaps sitting back for a tight match.

When the report did come, it must have surprised everybody who was fishing, and probably more so the organising officials— not a single bream had been caught along the whole of the 144-peg match length!

I told our runner to rest while I thought out the situation. As far as I could tell, all the teams had approached the match cautiously; in fact some of the Northern outfits had loose fed the slow-moving swims in an attempt to catch fish.

I reasoned that there was no excuse at all for the bream not to have shown in limited quantity after two hours of the match. Instinct told me that we must expect little, if any, improvement during the remaining three hours.

I was prepared to take a gamble. We knew there was an abundance of pike in the Rinn, in common with all Irish waters, and we had experimented with a method trying to catch these fish. This was to offer two white maggots and a large worm on the hook, and twitch it back along the river bed. I felt this was definitely worth a try, at least for the next hour, and sent the runner off to relay the decision to the rest of the team. He left me at a fair pace and I was left with the knowledge that within twenty minutes all the team members would be furnished with the revised plan.

The victorious Cofton Hackett team after disposing of Oundle and the rest in the 1975 National Winter League final (*Angling Times*)

An hour later and John appeared again, moving even more quickly. He was quite excited, and reported that there had still been no bream caught, but one of the Cofton side, John Rider, had landed a 6lb pike, and four or five other members had caught smaller samples.

He revealed that the other teams were starting to adopt similar tactics, thus endorsing our theory that a change was justified. We finished the match with a total of seventeen pike to our credit, and, just to cap it all, Alan Clarke had captured for us the only bream of the match.

The measure of sport produced in that final can be assessed by the fact that John Rider's pike of 6lb 11½oz put him in first place and Alan Clarke's bream, at 2lb 4oz was enough to gain the second individual position. Our master weight was 16lb 1½oz, made up of those seventeen pike, one bream and a few big-mouthed perch.

116

Whittlesea, a pedigree bream team if ever there was one, was the runner-up with 9lb 10oz.

Cofton had not achieved a brilliant weight, and it was certainly not an orthodox victory. But the performance proved the strength of the team's adaptability. Once again we had assessed the situation early in the match, and had out-foxed all our rivals.

As a team we knew that it was no fluke, but as in the case of our previous victory, we still felt that we had not gained the respect of the English match fraternity because of the unusual tactics which we had employed. What we badly needed was an orthodox, no-holds-barred contest to stamp our rights firmly on the winter-league game.

Probing back to that particular final, though, a popular question would be, whatever happened to the Rinn bream?

There is no close season in Ireland, and English anglers had very little experience in the mid-1960s of coarse fishing during the month of May. They were unaware of the fact that the fish travel greatly in search of spawning grounds and, as a result, rivers reputed to hold large populations become devoid of fish at the crucial time. This was exactly what had happened.

Nowadays, of course, with much more experience behind them of fishing Irish waters at this time of year, anglers tend to arrange their visits, and contests, in the areas where they know fish will be present.

After two less successful campaigns, we were again on the Irish trail in 1971 after once more beating off all challengers in the West Midlands League. This time the final was to be held on the Plassey section of the River Shannon and this indeed looked very much like the venue for which we had been waiting.

Arriving at the water during the late afternoon before match day, 'fish-at-all-cost' anglers from other teams were at the waterside within minutes of unpacking their tackle to confirm that the stretch held lots of bream.

We were then much more experienced as a bream team, especially in Irish waters, and we had again flown our bait over, not confident of relying on the local supplies.

Our team walked the match stretch from end to end and it certainly looked full of potential. But it was difficult to pinpoint the areas which might produce the best catches, which meant that every competitor could go into the match with the hope of good sport.

It was a very wide river, eighty to a hundred yards in parts, and the depth varied, though eight to ten feet could be found at most pegs. The pace was placid; in fact, it was copybook bream water.

We were by then very well aware that at this type of venue the only real formula to apply was one of attack, relying on the big weights to carry through less productive returns. Not for us the cautious approach where the potential of each peg is assessed, and tactics varied to suit the swim. We were all going flat-out for bream. In fact the venue looked that good we thought we might obtain eight good weights from our twelve-man assault.

Not for the first time, worms were going to be our main bait, and some 300 were cut up and mixed in the groundbait. At the start of the match each of our swims received a good ten pounds of the mix. If casters had been the fashionable bait in those days, I am sure that here was the type of swim which would have taken a gallon in any match.

None of us were expecting an immediate reaction because bream are bream, and even these Irish bream, though uninhibited feeders most of the time, are not normally con-fronted with the sort of barrage which we were giving them in that particular contest. The idea behind this generous feed pattern was, of course, that with so many anglers fishing the river at the same time, a mass of bait in the swim would hold the fish there for the rest of the match, once they had arrived.

With an hour of the final gone, bream started to show in most areas, in fact only the two extreme ends of the stretch seemed to be unproductive. This affected only a handful of competitors.

There were vast amounts of fish in the middle parts of the length where we had Austin Clissett working with a 9ft swing-tip rod and catching his fair share. Alan Clarke, another of our men, was also well among bream, and opposite him Hughie Boulter

118

was also busy netting fish. I was catching at a steady pace.

Johnny Coles, again running the bank, informed me that our bold tactics were reaping benefits, even though during the early stages the more cautious anglers in other teams had attracted the first bites. But with the match well under way the Cofton men were settling the fish down in large numbers. I must admit that before the final whistle sounded we were assured of another National Winter League victory.

We had put together quite a number of good weights, and the icing was really put on the cake when Austin Clissett, aided by several helping hands, dragged his huge catch to the scales. This was a sensation, the first 100lb match catch ever recorded by an English matchman, his actual weight being 101lb 6oz, easily a new event record.

Our winning weight was also a best ever, at 276lb 13½oz, and streets ahead of the field. For the first time we had achieved a result which even our greatest critics accepted as a performance of the highest order.

By 1975 winter-league involvement had shown tremendous growth, and, year by year, it was becoming harder to win. Semi-finals had become commonplace in the season's programme, and even the standard in our West Midlands League was very much higher.

The Birmingham-based Starlets outfit became the team to be reckoned with, and having removed this threat, we were off to the semi-final on the Warwickshire Avon at Eckington. Unlike in previous years, when the next stage would have been a trip to Ireland, the successful semi-finalists were to battle for the national crown much nearer home, at Coombe Abbey Lake, near Coventry, a change decided upon because of the troubles in Ireland.

Back to the semi-final, however, and this was indeed a strong line-up in which we saw our main rivals as Oundle, a team born and bred in bream country.

Eckington being a local venue for our team, we were able to enjoy many practice sessions. This was indeed a luxury, but the problem with all luxuries is they are not always accepted for what they are.

We knew that Eckington was a good bream water, even during March when the semi-final was to take place, but, having limitless time to spend at the venue, we started to look for alternative methods to have 'up our sleeves'.

Quite unintentionally we had prepared a very complicated team plan. We believed we knew the bream locations, and team members drawn in those areas were to fish for them. In the other swims which we considered barren in terms of bream, the plan was to try and catch bleak as a make-weight species.

On match day we were quietly confident that we had covered all approaches, and made for our pegs in the full knowledge of what we had to do at our different berths.

There was a big turnout of spectators, and after about two hours it became obvious from bankside chat that bream were being caught in odd numbers from the most unlikely places! Our cautious tactics had put us down the field and right in trouble. Although the odd member of our team drawn in the bream areas had caught a fish or two, we were pursuing a very negative approach overall. This called for a re-think, similar to that on the Rinn a few years earlier. We had to get out of trouble, and quickly!

I told the runner to advise each team member to scrap the bleak tactics and get after the bream. Fortunately, we had all groundbaited the far-bank area, so on went the little red worms and away we went.

With some ten minutes of the match left, Ivan Marks, such a good judge of a contest, came behind me and said we needed another bream to go through to the final, and no sooner had he said it than my tip curved around. I was playing a near three-pounder. But it seemed ages before the fish slipped over the rim of the net, and it was only just before the final whistle sounded.

Not knowing the water, Oundle had employed 'bream or bust' tactics, the right method on the day, and just pipped us at the post for first place. But we had sneaked into second position and so booked our place in the Coombe Abbey final. But without that late change of tactics we would have finished nowhere.

The final at Coombe Abbey created a lot of interest, one reason being that it was the first major contest of the new season. The press, perhaps rightly so, were naming Oundle as marginal favourites to win despite the fact that Cofton was the established Winter League outfit of the time with three national titles under our belt. The argument was that all this had been achieved on Irish waters and the critics maintained that we had not proved ourselves at home in England. There was also the important factor that Oundle had been smart enough to beat us on our home location at Eckington in the semi-final. What the critics did not know, though, was how we made that disastrously wrong approach for such a long period of that match.

The day of the big match finally arrived and our team assembled at headquarters armed with an ample supply of gozzers, squatts and groundbait. Betting was very close, Oundle being quoted at 2–1, and ourselves at 5–2.

Our plan was to feed five or six egg-sized balls of groundbait laced with squatts and casters at a distance of forty yards from the bank, and swing-tip a size 20 hook to 1lb bottom with a 5ft tail, using a ¾oz bomb to 2½lb reel line. Gozzers were to be the hookbait, the general opinion of the team being that two small baits would be the right approach.

As the match got under way our catapults were put to use, firing the groundbait out to the fishing area. Our attempt to clinch our fourth national-league victory, and our first on English waters, had begun.

As with all bream matches, progress was slow at the start but eventually bream were being slipped into the waiting keepnets. A number of fish were foul-hooked as, being the first few days of the season, the bream were moving fairly high in the water and not looking for anglers' baits. Few of these foul-hooked fish arrived at the nets, however, for Coombe Abbey bream are big, and, as the virgin pandock beds formed considerable obstruction to the competitors, breakages were common.

Two members of our team, Ken Smith and Paul Evans, were drawn almost opposite each other and were enjoying good sport. At the entrance to the lake on the public bank, Ron Lees was also finding fish for Cofton, but we were certainly not having things all our own way as the Oundle team men were also catching their fair share.

Few bankside punters were willing to stake too much on one team or the other, and only the scales were going to have to decide the issue.

We received a good start from Ken Smith who scaled more than 30lb. Then Paul Evans chipped in with a fine 25lb catch, and Ron Lees followed up with 20lb. I fell just short of this with a high 19lb, and with very good backing weights we were able to amass more than 100lb.

Meanwhile Oundle, our conquerors from Eckington, were busy putting their scores together, but they finished short of our three-figure total, having to settle for second place.

That day we had beaten one of the country's top bream outfits, in fact some people would say the No 1 side, at their own game. At last we had proved that we were to be feared not only on Irish waters but also at home venues.

Cofton's record of four victories is a target for every winter-league outfit in the country and one which I believe will stand for a very long time. At the same time I am hoping that before not too long we can extend our total of victories to five.

This target might well have been achieved in the following year when Cofton again won their way through to the final at the same Coombe venue. But then we were pipped at the post by Dorking. There was some consolation for us, however, in providing the individual winner—Ken Giles, with a mammoth catch of more than fifty pounds.

Ken Smith (Cofton Hackett) with his top catch from the National Winter League final held at Coombe Abbey lake, 1975 (*Angling Times*)

8
The Birmingham
Angling Festival

The Birmingham Angling Festival differs from our other match-fishing events in several respects and is the only promotion of its kind staged by a local authority. It embraces highly competitive team and individual open championships and also includes junior and senior citizen title events.

The Festival is sponsored by Mitchells & Butlers, the Birmingham brewers, and their donation is increased almost annually. This has led to the happy position of the Festival having the richest team prize in the country, a handsome pay-out fast approaching the £2,000 mark.

It is this team section which creates by far the greater spectator interest, and the majority of participating anglers prefer success in this championship rather than gain individual honours.

Teams travel hundreds of miles from all over the country to take part in this atmospheric showpiece, and the promoters are always assured of a big entry.

The venues for the preliminary rounds are the park pools owned by Birmingham Corporation and all are sited within the city boundaries. Prior to the introduction of this competition these were the training grounds for the city's younger anglers but they were almost totally disregarded by senior sportsmen who sought waters much farther afield for their competitive fishing.

Today, of course, the picture is far different. When the draw is announced, usually late during the close season, competitors champ at the bit in anticipation of 16 June which gives them the green light to practice for the coming parks events.

The structure of the competition is interesting in itself because the venues used all have varying peg capacities. A team can be drawn at a pool with only twenty-four pegs, in other words four teams each of six anglers, or, at the other extreme, they can be sited at water such as Edgbaston Reservoir which in past years has accommodated as many as twenty teams. But because of this disparity an acceptable balance is achieved by working on a percentage basis for teams progressing to the next round. For instance, from the first round, 50 per cent of all teams taking part at the various pools go forward, irrespective of the size of the line-up. Their next hurdle is the semi-final and recently this has been staged at the well-known Edgbaston fishery, an excellent roach water which was selected for the filming of the BBC 2 television series, *Hooked*.

From here, progress to the final is far harder to achieve, and to keep interest alive it is essential for a team to finish in the first three of its group which usually comprises some twelve or fourteen teams.

There are four of these semi-finals, fished over a period of two to three weeks, and quite obviously the standard of competition is now much higher.

From these semi-finals, twelve successful teams go through to the grand final. All the preliminary rounds are evening events about 2- or 2½-hours long, but the final is usually a 4-hour contest and is fished on the closing Saturday as a climax to the whole Festival. Given good weather, this match can be guaranteed to attract the largest crowds—up to several thousands.

For me the Festival has always been an event of real enjoyment, no doubt increased by the considerable success which I have been fortunate in achieving with the Cofton Hackett team.

Before sponsorship added lustre to the competition, the event was for several years previously more of a prestige competition, organised under the title of the Birmingham Parks Knockout. This was in the late 60s when I was fortunate enough to skipper Cofton to three consecutive victories.

During that period competition was at quite a high level but because of the limited prize money—the winning team received a moderate £36—it wasn't practicable for teams based long distances from the Midlands to participate.

After Cofton's 'hat-trick' we felt it only right in the interests of the competition to refrain from competing for two or three years. But when the event was re-launched as the Birmingham Festival with the backing of Mitchells & Butlers, thus considerably widening its scope, it attracted teams from all parts of the country, providing competition of the highest standard. It was under these circumstances that Cofton made its re-entry to the event, in 1975.

Our quest for the trophy started with a first-round draw at Salford Park, at the city's second-largest pool, situated immediately beneath the famous Spaghetti Junction.

On paper, it looked a pretty easy task for us to qualify for the Edgbaston Reservoir semi-final, but it was made that little bit more tricky because the Salford fish population comprised mainly two heavy-weight species—tench and carp. There were very few roach and perch there in 1975. The tench were handsome fish, with many weighing two to four pounds, while the carp were even larger with eight- and nine-pounders quite common.

Our problem was that teams who might latch on to these big fish would be extremely difficult to pull back, especially as the preliminary round was a mere two-hours long. Another factor certainly not in our favour was that both carp and tench show little respect for bait presentation and gossamer tackle. Often they are more attracted to two or three large maggots fished with a heavy line by the less knowledgeable anglers. Because of their crude tactics, their chances of netting these bigger fish were so much better than ours.

It is perhaps easy to say that we all had the option to use this heavy type of rig, but, as all matchmen know, it is hard to convince oneself that a size 14 hook to 2½lb bs line will attract bites on a hot summer's night with not a breath of wind on the water. We were sure that because of lack of weed and underwater snags the right approach would be to fish for bites with light lines and small hooks. It was the only way we could tackle the match with any peace of mind and confidence.

We used single-maggot bait on a size 20 hook to 1lb bottom, and we fished about 2ft overdepth with 3AAA waggler floats some three to four rod lengths out from the bank. We fed our swims with brown groundbait laced with squatts and a few casters.

At the halfway point we were far behind, not one of our team having contacted any respectably sized fish, but the later period was much more fruitful for us as Barrie Brookes, Max Winters and Lloyd Davies all managed to locate an odd tench or two. Even so we were able to finish only third behind some big fish, and were glad of the substantial number of qualifiers, six in all, who were to go through to the semi-final.

This second stage of the competition was scheduled to take place three weeks later, at Edgbaston Reservoir. The final would be held at the picturesque Cannon Hill Park where the line-up was reduced to eight teams. This meant that if a team was to qualify for the final it would have to take either first or second place in one of the four semi-finals.

We used the interval up to the semi-final practising hard at a somewhat stubborn Edgbaston Reservoir. The summer of 1975 was exceptionally hot, with temperatures well into the 90s, and this was beginning to affect the productivity of this big-city pool. However, from our practice sessions, a method slowly emerged to produce satisfying results. This was to offer a caster on a size 18 hook to 1lb trace and 2½lb reel line, fished with a 2-swan waggler float. The roach seemed to respond as we wanted.

These were not large catches, around a dozen-and-a-half fish ranging between three and six ounces apiece from the better areas during a two- to three-hour stint.

As is so often the case with waters not fishing at their best, the problem was that certain areas became almost barren, and quite often a small section of the reservoir will hold the key for a successful team.

On semi-final night the Cofton man to shoulder the responsibility of getting us through was Barrie Brookes. He drew a peg
opposite the ballroom at the Edgbaston water, which had been
the most consistent section during the run-up to the match.

The rest of us were fishing for a mere pound or so, some of us
even for bites. It was a flat-calm night following a scorching-hot
day and we all knew this was going to be a hard nut to crack.

As the match progressed, reports circulating around the pool
that the predicted area was indeed producing fish seemed to
justify all the pre-match comment. The trouble was, as far as
Cofton was concerned, our man in the productive area was not
opening up a winning margin. With half of the match gone, three
or four anglers in the area had about the same weight.

During the second part of the match the competitors had to
fish through a violent thunderstorm which made progress very
difficult. I caught only one fish during that period, an 8oz roach.

As the match drew to a close it was very difficult to predict
which of the competing teams would go through to the Cannon
Hill Park final because the weights were so low.

The favourites were local specialists Warley and District, and
as our man Barrie Brookes was beaten on his right-hand flank by
one of their team, it seemed they would get the decision. They
did, with over seven pounds and we followed them in second
place with the very low team weight for this wonderful pool of
about six pounds.

However, the important thing was we were through to the
final, and from then on Cannon Hill was to engage our full
attention, though our actual practice with groundbait at the
water was restricted to a single day.

Because of the unusually hot spell, pleasure-anglers had been
barred from using groundbait at the water in an effort to preserve
fish life.

For our practice session, we decided to fish the same hours,
2–6pm, as in the actual match, and the day we chose was a
Tuesday. The final was to take place on the following Saturday,
and all we could do was to keep our fingers crossed that similar

conditions prevailed for the remainder of the week. The only differing factor would be that during our work-out we would have to contend with a flotilla of rowing boats around the pool, but these would not be allowed during the final.

We positioned ourselves at six imaginary pegs and drew for numbers in an effort to simulate proper match conditions. We decided to fish two matches, each of two hours, on different sections of the forty-eight peg pool, and for the first hour we all struggled, catching only the odd fish with long intervals of inactivity. Temperatures were soaring into the 90s, and perhaps we were unreasonable in seeking very much improvement on that sluggish catch rate.

But one of our party, Tony Scott, was not content with this. Quite suddenly he started to produce roach frequently. They weren't big fish but nonetheless they were potentially exciting on a rather dull day. I found it quite impossible to sit there and watch Tony catch these fish, so I went over to his peg and saw that he had forsaken all maggot baits in favour of a bread punch. Quickly I advised our other four anglers of the situation and they were soon scrounging pieces of bread and sorting through their tackle boxes in search of little-used bread punches.

The change of tactics brought an unbelievable transformation. All our team started catching fish straightaway, and in no time it became apparent that we had hit upon a successful method which had to be protected from strolling rivals!

We fished out the hour, weighed our catches, and, full of confidence, drew stumps to await Saturday's final.

During the next few days we did some strolling of our own and were delighted to see teams such as Leicester and the Starlets struggling to make more conventional maggot methods work.

Eventually Saturday arrived and, as we had hoped, conditions remained extreme, very hot and still, in fact ideal for our bread-punch method.

Cannon Hill is a shallow pool, man-made with a depth rarely in excess of 3½ feet. It is not a big water and all pegs can be fished with a 3BB canal-type set-up.

The floats we used were of the cane variety with a thin skin of balsa, as shown in Fig 14. Lead wire semi-loaded the float so that all that was needed on the line were two locating shots each side of the float and a No 10 micro some 10 inches above the size 20 fine-wire hook. This was attached to 1lb line, with 1½lb strength used on the reel.

The fishing depth was critical. It needed to be set so that the bread was positioned one inch off the bed of the pool, while the other vital ingredient for success was considered to be ground-bait. This had been finely riddled, though not in large quantity, each of our six anglers expecting to use about two pounds. A

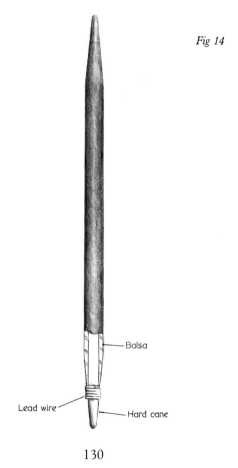

Fig 14

Balsa

Lead wire

Hard cane

130

tablespoonful of large breadcrumbs was added to the groundbait and mixed thoroughly. This was kept dry, ready for mixing with water just prior to the start of the match. Even then it would be kept on the dry side so that a percentage of it would float on the surface of the pool for a short period, thus creating a situation where particles dropped through the water for some minutes after being thrown.

The official draw took place, and tactics were a closely guarded secret. Ivan Marks's Leicester team was keen to learn how we had fared with our practice, but as we arrived at our pegs no information had leaked out. We tackled up for the match being very careful to keep all slices of bread well out of sight, also any item of tackle, such as a bread board, or punch, that would give any inkling of our approach.

This attitude was vital because there was going to be little doubt that the sun-drenched pool would deteriorate very quickly indeed as the match progressed. Any team getting off to a good start would create a situation where it was impossible for them to be pulled back.

Eventually we all got under way, myself from a nice-looking peg, No 43 opposite the island at the entry to the pool. I tossed in a piece of groundbait the size of a 5p piece to within a yard of the island wall, a simple cast of some two-and-a-half rod lengths.

I punched my bread and impaled this on to my size 20 hook, flicked it across to the deposit of groundbait, well marked by the floating particles.

I was using the same float which I had employed for our practice session, and I was surprised to see it submerge almost immediately, leading me to believe for a short time that perhaps the wrong shots had been used to position the float on the line. I swept the rod to the side, more or less as a practice strike, and was again surprised to see the tip arc round, and a 2oz roach come quickly to hand.

My shotting was perfectly in order, and for the next hour fish came quickly, one after another. My team colleague Max Winters was having a similar reaction from the fish, though he

The author with the Cofton team which he skippered to victory in the 1976 Birmingham Angling Festival team championships

was not catching quite so quickly as myself, being at a swim well in the open and not so favourable in the hot conditions.

In fact, the whole of our team were catching fish and, exactly as had been predicted, a deterioration set in just before mid-match. But the damage had been done by Cofton. We had opened up a massive lead under the conditions, and only one of the pool's large resident carp was going to give any of the other seven teams a chance to gain first place.

As the match ended there were large crowds anxious to witness the weigh-in of this first sponsored Festival, and when the scales reached my peg the best weight from the five competitors who had already weighed their catches was just over a pound.

My fish took the needle to just short of four pounds. All match fishing is relevant to conditions and venue potential, and four pounds from this piece of water on a day of so much heat was one of my best performances in a long angling career.

The rest of the Cofton team backed up with good weights, and we more than doubled the catch of the second-placed team.

An hour after the match we filed up to receive our trophies together with a handsome cheque. We were the first champions of the new-style Birmingham Angling Festival, and our mood was such that we had no intention of losing this coveted crown.

Because of the huge success of the inaugural Festival there was an extremely large entry for all events in 1976, including the Open Team Championship which we were bidding to win for a second successive year.

We were drawn at Edgbaston Reservoir in the opening round, one of twenty-two teams striving for a place in the semi-final. On paper, the effort needed to qualify on this very orthodox town-centre roach fishery did not seem too great. After all, we had only to finish in the top half of the field as 50 per cent of the line-up would be going through.

But the match assumed a more important dimension for us with the inclusion of the fine Leicester side, whom we had conquered in the previous year's final. They would be fishing a piece of water much more suited to their style.

Though showing some improvement on the previous year, the reservoir was still inconsistent over the match course and again the bulk of our fish could be expected to come from only a third of our team. After two or three practice sessions we were convinced that the right method for success was identical to that employed in 1975. We rounded off preparations and looked forward to the duel with our Leicester rivals.

Match night came around and in a way it was a relaxed evening. With the roach responding, even only in limited areas, and a man every twenty-two pegs, there was little likelihood of our being drawn off the fish in all sections.

Everything went more or less to plan, the fortunate man for us being Ken Giles who was drawn in front of the ballroom and had a very fruitful evening's fishing. In the two-hour match he put together the very creditable weight of 11lb 6½oz, consisting entirely of roach. It was a fine exhibition of fishing given in front of a large crowd assembled to watch the battle between these two well-known teams.

However, though fortunate in having Ken's winning individual weight, we were handicapped by two very poor draws, both resulting in dry nets, and they trimmed our total weight to 18lb 4oz. Leicester showed more consistency, both in the draw and performance, and, using similar methods, just edged in front of us with 19lb 10oz.

Nevertheless, we were on route to the semi-final, though this was going to be a much tougher affair at the Salford Park venue, a water notorious for its big fish and one quite capable of causing a major upset for teams questing for a place in the final. This was confirmed in practice as we found very few small fish, such as roach and perch, but found that larger tench and carp dominated the build-up to this important hurdle.

After several visits there emerged a pattern that on any given night either one, two or three large fish, tench in the three- to four-pound class and carp up to as much as seventeen pounds would find their way into anglers' nets. It was obvious that a team fishing merely for roach and perch was going to stand little chance because only two teams were to qualify, and it would need only two of these large fish to be landed by separate sides to decide the issue.

We had to find a way of catching these bigger tench and carp or, if it proved easier, work out some theory whereby we could stop them feeding while we went for the more reliable smaller species.

We finally banked on the latter tactic, and it was a somewhat evil plan conceived by the six Cofton members. We discovered from our practice sessions that the best tempter for these large fish was luncheon meat. We though it worth a gamble to place about two pounds of finely cubed meat in a good area in each of our swims. With a bit of luck the result would be overfeeding by the tench and carp. By introducing thousands of meat cubes into the water, the odds against a single piece of meat impaled on a hook resulting in the capture of a fish would be lengthened considerably.

When we finally lined up for the match and the whistle started us off lumps of meat were flying everywhere within seconds. It didn't make us a lot of friends, but that wasn't the intention. Our singular approach was to secure a place in the 1976 final with a chance to retain the trophy.

I had worked out that the most dangerous period for us would be the early minutes of the match when feeding carp and tench would be showing a gluttonous approach to this sudden windfall of feed. I believed that they would quickly eat their fill, then languish with little further interest in baits for the remainder of the match. This worked a treat as a plan, but I'm afraid that it stopped any chance of good weights. We crept through to the final in second place behind Amery Unionists with mini-weights of 1lb 2oz and 1lb 4oz respectively. Ivan Marks' Leicester team, our conquerors in the first round, had fallen completely for this big-fish elimination ploy. They had based their attack on the super-heavies and finished bottom of the fourteen teams with just one ounce.

So we were through to the Cannon Hill final for the second year running and would be competing against seven other successful sides including the highly rated Birmingham Starlets senior team.

As in previous years, we were allowed one practice session with groundbait, but we could visit the water any time to try alternative methods not requiring the use of cereal.

It was noticed during our visits that fish at Cannon Hill had become interested in the caster. This was markedly different to the previous year when the bread punch seemed to be the main attraction.

By the time our official practice day came along the caster had made so much impact with us that we were thinking if we could couple a good start with the bread punch, this being a noted instant method, we would have a fine combination and one which could give us the advantage over other caster-motivated teams.

With this in mind we found ourselves six swims to fish, intending to work the normal match hours of 2–6pm, and made our first approach with the bread punch. But this opening sally produced only two small roach.

Then we switched to our second method, the caster, which we firmly believed was to be our banker approach on match day. A few loose casters were put out into the swim and a 2AAA waggler float with a fine insert tip was cast about 2½-rod lengths out from the bank. A No 10 shot was positioned 10 inches from the hook with a No 8 placed midway between this and the float, the waggler being set 12 inches overdepth in the constant 3 feet of water. A single caster was impaled on a size 18 barbless hook, and fish started to take the bait from all six of us almost immediately. Roach in the three- to four-ounce class and even small bream soon found their way into our nets.

We ended the practice session with mixed feelings because the tactic which we thought would give us an opening advantage, the bread punch, had failed completely, yet the caster had certainly turned up trumps.

The problem was that in 1976 caster bait was all the rage and it was not going to be a secret to many, if any, of the competing teams. As with the first round, it seemed that expertise would again be the winning factor.

The day of the final soon came around and as the teams assembled at the attractive Cannon Hill Park venue it was a lovely afternoon which, although not exactly beneficial to the fishing, was certainly appreciated by the large crowd gathered to witness this decider to end the Festival.

The destiny of the coveted Birmingham Parks Trophy according to bankside speculation seemed to be about equally divided between the Starlets and our Cofton team, and this is exactly how we envisaged the set-up. We drew our pegs, wished each other good luck, and off we went, all hoping to make it two victories in succession.

Clive Smith with his catch which helped Cofton to win the team event in the 1976 Birmingham Angling Festival

It might have been because of our win in the previous year but that match has extra-happy memories and I can rarely remember being as keen as I was on that particular day.

I drew Peg 3 which was at the park entrance and lacking in any cover. It was probably the narrowest peg on the water, some thirty yards wide from bank to bank, but at least it gave me a good view of opposing team members on the other bank.

Having dispensed with the bread punch as an opener, we all planned to start with the caster and fish this right through the match. I cast to the middle of my swim, about fifteen yards out, sunk my line and fired six to eight casters around the float. I repeated this every two or three minutes and with about five minutes gone my float dipped from sight and a four-ounce roach was on the way to the net.

I caught a second roach after another five minutes, and slowly a procession of similar fish found its way into my keepnet.

Meanwhile a large crowd was gathering around a peg near the windmill where our new man, Ken Smith, was well among a shoal of bream after having earlier caught a few roach. He was catching steadily and looked set for what could be a big weight for this hard-fished water.

On the far bank progress was slow, though my colleague Max Winters gave the spectators something to watch when he played and landed a carp around the three-pound mark.

Half way through the match we were well in command. It seemed that Cannon Hill was our lucky venue, and the second half was a replica of the first. I kept on catching, Ken Smith added more bream to his tally, and to bring down the curtain on what was obviously going to be a very successful final for us, Max Winters latched on to another carp. This was similar to his earlier fish and he hooked it just before the finishing whistle, which meant that the spectators were going to have extra time to watch as he brought the fish to submission. He had a fifteen-minute limit after the match in which to net the carp so took his time, eventually sliding it over his landing aid with a couple of minutes to spare.

Eventually Max weighed in 7lb 14oz, the second-best weight of the day, and I was quite pleased with my return of 5lb 12oz comprising about sixty roach, and making third best in the match.

However, the star of the day was undoubtedly Ken Smith who finished with a quite spectacular catch of 14lb 9½oz, the best match figures which had up to then ever been set at the Cannon Hill water. He caught some fine fish, and the performance was an encouragement to the many youngsters who had watched the match in the hope of gaining some knowledge of how to fish their local pools.

Our other three team men, Ken Giles, Lloyd Davies and Barrie Brookes all came up with reasonable backing weights and we finished with a very fine aggregate of nearly thirty-two pounds, this being more than three times the weight of any other team's catch!

As predicted, Birmingham Starlets were runners-up, but I am sure they were surprised by the margin of our victory.

It was indeed satisfying for us to receive the trophy for the second successive year—no mean feat from an original entry of well over 100 teams.

Then it was on to 1977, and our obvious intention was to go for the hat-trick. In pursuit of this we made a brilliant start in the opening round at Edgbaston Reservoir.

Once again the Festival was very well patronised and there were no fewer than twenty-four teams in this first-round clash so pegs were shortened to a mere eight or ten yards.

Cofton were again up against the powerful Starlets outfit who would no doubt be seeking revenge for last year's crushing defeat in the final, but once more we were in top form and annihilated the opposition with a record-breaking team total of 45lb 3oz. This was a performance made more creditable by the limited room in which we had to operate.

The victory took us through to the second round and again Salford Park where we managed to clinch second qualifying place, a large tench gaining the match for the winning team which proved too much for us to pull back on a water fishing well below par. But the important thing was that we were through to the final, and the hat-trick was on the cards.

Our main opposition again came from the Starlets, and it was their team man Barry Fulford—who latched on to a foul-hooked three-pound bream with only minutes of the match left—who was our undoing. He slid his landing-net under the fish in the dying seconds, and it clinched the decision for the Starlets, leaving Cofton in second place just over a pound behind.

Cannon Hill had finally turned on us. How we would have loved to have secured our third successive victory.

9

My Favourite Match

More than two decades of match fishing have obviously left me with a host of memories involving innumerable contests, many of them successful but others not quite so rewarding. Good catches always stand out in the mind. There have been scores of problems to solve, but some situations were sufficiently mystifying to defy solution, yet in their own way they too have added to the attraction of the sport.

As all match anglers are aware, there are the bleak periods when good draws and the accompanying satisfactory results are just not forthcoming. Adverse weather conditions, such as snow, ice and floods often interrupt our game and make it difficult to pursue. Then, of course, there are the dreaded twelve weeks of 'internment' when, in compliance with the laws of the land, in the greater part of the country we are not allowed to fish in the way which we wish.

We tend to look back on the better days as if seeking some compensation for the frustrating periods. I am perhaps fortunate in this respect in having an abundance of memories to call upon, but the one at the top of my list, and it must rate as the most satisfying and enjoyable day's fishing I have ever experienced, is, perhaps surprisingly, a 100-peg run-of-the-mill open event which I fished on the banks of the superb River Severn at picturesque Stourport.

That match took place in November 1976, on a river in perfect condition. It was a Saturday event, and followed only a week or two after a West Midlands League match at the same venue where I had won with a catch of 37½lb of roach.

This was an exceptional catch of roach and it came during a period when I was enjoying considerable success at the Stourport venue. Over two years I recorded a ratio of more than one victory out of every two matches which I fished at the water!

One major factor contributing to my fond memories of Stourport was the atmosphere which surrounded these mid-1970s contests. The river was always capable of producing all-roach catches among the winning bags, and because of excellent coverage by the angling press, the events did not go unnoticed. The turn-outs always contained large numbers of nationally known anglers.

Competition was fierce, making success that much more satisfying, but the social side of the events also added much to their attraction, the draw being at the local Showboat Inn where welcome refreshments were available.

These were afternoon matches, usually 4½ hours long, being fished from 12.30–5pm. On that particularly memorable October day, having enjoyed such a splendid run of success on the water, topped by my recent very fine weight in the League match, I was especially keen to endorse it all by giving another rewarding performance.

The match course held 100 pegs, though with the high quality of fishing the organisers could have sold ten times as many. Of these I rated only twenty as being incapable of producing a catch good enough to make the top six, with twenty-five potentially 'winning' swims.

I drew a peg two swims from the bottom of the length, immediately above the caravan park. I had not previously fished the swim but when I saw it I was immediately convinced that it should hold a fair head of roach.

A bush was nicely situated at the downstream end of my swim and the bank position itself was comfortable, being low on to the water. Moreover, the pace indicated to me that the depth was sufficient to hold roach at that time of year, just prior to the winter months.

I tackled up with no little enthusiasm, selecting a 2BB stick float and shotting it in the accepted Stourport fashion with a No 10 shot eight to ten inches from the hook and small shot equally spread from there to the float. These shot were of staggered sizes with a No 8 immediately above the size 10, and the largest one to be used at this particular peg a No 6 as I believed the water to be about five-feet deep.

I set the float at about seven feet, giving me an extra two feet to play with, allowing the sort of presentation needed to trick these quality Stourport fish.

My reel line was 1½lb bs with a 1lb hooklength, to which was attached a size 18 crystal-bend barbless hook. The bait, as always for this time of year, was caster with a liberal lacing of well-cooked hempseed. This was used as an attractor, fed in reasonable quantity on the starting whistle, say three or four good handfuls, and then mixed in equal proportions with casters in my bait apron.

I firmly believed before the match started that it was going to be a free-feeding roach-fishing affair for which I should require only one rod, and when the whistle signalled the 'off' I settled in my peg in a standing position, quite prepared for the customary thirty to forty minutes of inactivity as far as fish were concerned. However, during this pre-catching period there was much to be done as I believe it always takes a good hour when working with a stick float to adjust the balance for a satisfactory performance. Then there is the feeding pattern to pursue.

When I plumbed the depth I found it to be very close to my estimated five feet and having previously set my tackle in excess of this measurement, I minimised disturbance of the swim by making only one entry with the plumb bob.

I fixed a caster to the hook and started fishing, more at that stage in an exploratory manner rather than with any expectancy of catching fish. I was looking for the high spots in the swim, the sort of areas which could retain the loose feed which was cast in during the course of the match. But I was also watching for any snags which might be in the swim because the constant fouling of tackle on obstacles can be very off-putting for a feeding shoal of roach when the angler attempts to pull himself clear. However, I was extremely fortunate on that day, there being very little obstruction at all. In fact, it was what I like to term a very friendly peg and tailor-made for catching roach in that particular section of river.

In feeding the swim at regular intervals, though not heavily, my typical feed-rate per swim down was six to eight casters on the cast, then a further two or three tossed to the same position every ten to fifteen seconds after this. This was a left-handed operation to leave my right hand controlling the tackle. Only when I was re-baiting or landing a fish would both my hands be working on the same task.

During these late autumn months my intention has always been to fish as far overdepth as possible, slowing down the tackle to somewhere near half the speed of the current. Obviously, with this degree of retardment the angle between the float and the hook increases sharply, thus requiring a great extension of the distance between the two.

After some fine adjustments to my tackle, I was fishing at a depth between the float and the hook of nearly eight feet, three feet more than the true depth of the water.

I continually edged the float down the swim, at times stopping it completely and then running it through at varying speeds in an effort to simulate the hand-fed samples.

My first fish came, ideally, at the time I would have planned if I had perfect control of the situation. I don't like catching fish in matches straight from the 'off' for I believe that their confidence has not been gained at this time, and then they often make a quick retreat for safer pastures.

A lapse of some thirty minutes after the starting whistle would suggest that the fish have gained at least a certain degree of confidence in the feeding pattern being presented, and the removal of the occasional roach does, I hope, go largely unnoticed by the remainder of the preoccupied feeding shoal.

The author with the winning bag of fish from his favourite match, Stourport 1976

After another ten minutes or so, a second roach of six to eight ounces was fed into my waiting net. The feeding pattern remained the same but at that juncture I was still fishing far too long a swim in terms of compiling a substantial weight. I was constantly looking for a situation in which the passage of my float would be considerably shortened to no more than about four yards because it is when operating at these shorter distances that the real damage can be done.

During the next hour I caught about four pounds of fish, confirming their continuing presence in the swim, but I still had that uneasy feeling of not being able to work the peg into a sufficiently fast catch rate to gain a high match place on this excellent fishing day.

When the next couple of hours continued on the same lines my frustration increased as I dearly wanted to speed up the demise of the shoal. Apart from that I was having a good match and do not recall losing a single hook. Moreover, the spectators did not hinder me in trying to localise the fish in a more convenient catching area.

There was just about an hour to go and some 12lb in my net when I felt that decisions had to be made. In no way could I see 16lb being enough to win, and this seemed to be my ultimate catch if I kept to my present course and caught at the same rate.

I needed to take some sort of gamble in an effort to speed up my catch-rate. As it was such a calm day, giving the fish a good view of me, I surmised that my standing position was deterring the fish from coming closer. So I settled my box in the peg and, unusually for me, decided to fish the remainder of the match in a sitting position.

The transformation was quite startling. Almost immediately I was catching roach just beyond the end of my rod! Not only were the intervals between each fish cut down drastically but also larger roach moved in and seemed keen to feed.

At this shorter distance, my rhythm was sweet and I well remember developing a knack of casting (perhaps a better description of such close-in action would be 'dropping') the tackle on the water and holding it tight until the float assumed a correct position, and just edging it through the 3–4ft course.

Very few of my runs down the swim failed to connect with a fish, and as so often happens on these 'blue riband' days there were occasional bonus fish from which there had been no visual bite indication through the float. These came when the tackle was being retrieved for the next cast.

During that final prolific hour I added more than 20lb to my catch to end with a total weight of 34lb 13½oz!

For 4½ hours I had enjoyed my most pleasurable match-fishing experience. But I don't think it would have impressed me so much if I had caught the fish during, say, the second or third hour. As with all sporting events, the ideal finish comes in the 'home straight'.

Exciting cup finals are won in the last seconds, great horse races are remembered for 'last ditch' efforts, and to me this Lyttelton Open contest was no exception for the same reason.

It seemed to me that I had nursed the peg, then plundered it in the closing stages, and as I left the bankside I felt that if I had continued fishing I would have found that a termination of sport wasn't far off. The swim had been paced out and I believe I had achieved a near 100 per cent return on its potential.

I won that match very comfortably and, with my previous big catch in the League match, had recorded two of the highest-ever roach weights to come from this well-known water. I remember them both very clearly, but the match I have just described holds that little bit of extra magic. It was an event which I cannot see ever being surpassed in terms of providing everything which fishing means to me.

10

The World Championships

By 1981 England's record in the World Championships had been one of ups and downs with several near-misses but disappointing in the fact that the home country had never won this top matchfishing crown.

I had personal experience of this disappointment in 1973 when I was a member of the team which finished third, albeit a creditable position, at Chalon-sur-Saône in France.

On this particular day the French must have been equally disappointed in being beaten by the Belgians, their arch-rivals, on their home water.

However, it was a grand experience for me to compete at international level, and evoked feelings which I could never have envisaged before. This was emphasised by the fact of fishing in foreign waters under continental organisation.

After this French sortie, I had to wait until 1980 for a recall to the England squad. This year the venue was the River Necker at Mannheim in West Germany, and my selection came as a real surprise mainly because this was an out-and-out pole venue, a method of which I had limited experience, especially with the long-pole designs.

We had two-weeks practice on the actual match course prior to the Championships, but unfortunately for the greater part of the first week I was severely handicapped by an insect sting and this considerably restricted my training programme.

When the day of the match arrived I was to act as assistant coach, working with our team manager, Stan Smith, to keep the fishing members of our team fully informed of what was happening along the match course.

That day England gained a superb result in finishing second, beaten only by the host-country, West Germany, with the mighty French anglers trailing behind us. I was fortunate in being selected by Stan Smith to fish in the Individual Championship event the following day, and recorded a weight of around fifteen pounds in the 2½-hour match.

I worked all through the match with a ten-metre pole, and my catch put me in tenth position, for which I received a delightful cut-glass tankard and a medal (awarded to the top twelve in this 1980 Individual World Championship).

But despite this great performance by the England team, we were, after twenty-four years, still seeking to win the coveted team award.

So it was with eager excitement that anglers throughout the land looked to the 1981 event, with its siting on English waters, as our big chance of at last gaining this elusive title. It was to be housed along the banks of the picturesque Warwickshire Avon, a mile or two downstream from Stratford, the first time this much-improved river had been chosen for the international event.

The waters selected for the match course comprised the Manor Farm stretch at the pretty village of Luddington, a fishery noted for its chub and, in a supporting role, dace. The swims along this length vary considerably, but in general it is typical up-river water with numerous shallow rushy-fringed glides of around three feet, interspersed by deeper runs.

Announcement of the six-strong squad to represent England was finally made—after wide speculation on the part of the media —late in May. And whilst in previous years this announcement had usually been followed by varying degrees of criticism about the selection, this time the grumbles and grouses were surprisingly few. It gave the impression that the selectors were on the right course for a team victory.

Together with England regulars Kevin Ashurst, already capped ten times, and Tony Scott with no fewer than seven previous appearances, the squad included myself for a third time, Dave Thomas earning his second cap, and two newcomers. These were, very predictably, John Dean and Max Winters—

both very familiar with the Avon and both having enjoyed immense success on the river in the preceding few years.

We assembled for the first time at the beginning of June to gain an early appraisal of the water. The session comprised a comfortable stroll along the match course, after which we retired to the Four Alls, a local hostelry. Here we were brought up to date with the work which had been going on in preparation for the match for the past couple of years or so, and we started to plan our general approach to the match.

Very much at the centre of these discussions was Stan Smith, who had been team manager for the past decade and with the event being staged in this country, had also been appointed International Events Manager.

It was decided that the squad members should visit the stretch from the start of the match season and familiarise themselves with the varying depths, flows, and other generalities.

The world match was scheduled for the weekend of 19–20 September, and two weeks prior to this a much more concentrated approach was planned. Over a period of three days the squad members were to fish a series of six-man matches, each of three-hours duration, in true Stan Smith style. With two separate sessions each day, it meant a total of six contests along the Championship water.

One factor about which we were pleased during our first few visits to the venue was in finding that the grading work carried out on the banks specially for the Championships seemed to have only negligible effect on the fish.

At this stage, in fact, fish were not difficult to catch, and it was soon evident that along the match stretch the stick float fished in conjunction with maggot hookbait among loose-fed samples was the most effective catching method.

The only alternative to this was the waggler float, to be employed as a follow-up to the stick-float attack, which would remove the fish quartered close in to the bank before they became unduly alarmed by the retrieving of far-bank tackle.

When our final three-day work-out came along all the squad

members were fishing with almost identical set-ups. And it did become apparent during these experimental days that a down-stream peg could usually be relied upon to produce a top weight.

At the end of the practice runs there was little mystery about the method which would be used by England. The sole bait to be considered was bronze maggot, fished with size 20 and 22 hooks to 1lb bs hooklength with either a stick or waggler float.

In the event of a stick float being used the reel line would be 1½lb bs, while with the waggler a breaking strain of just over two pounds was thought necessary.

These two methods were to be the complete armoury of the England team. Lead fishing as a supplementary approach could not be considered because this is banned under international rules.

It was heartening to us during the build-up to the match to see the visiting continental teams, albeit with their long poles and magical bloodworm and groundbait expertise, catching some fish but not putting together anything like a substantial catch.

Tension mounted as the week-end of the match approached and pressure built up around each angler. We had enjoyed such good summer conditions, the question now was, could this be maintained just for another week or so until the Championships? And would the vast crowds which were expected—prediction put the number at around 20,000—make any difference to the feeding habits of the ever-suspicious chub?

Another burning question among the squad members surrounded Stan Smith's selection of the five men who would fish. Who would be the one delegated to act as assistant team-coach? We were, of course, not to know this until twelve hours before the match.

All these factors added to the strain put upon the squad members as the big day drew nearer.

Two days prior to the Championships, on the Thursday, several of the squad walked the bank of the match course in a very happy frame of mind. The river looked in tip-top condition after the few showers of the previous week-end. These had freshened the water and undoubtedly led to a sharpening of the fishes' appetites.

But then came an abrupt and very unwelcome change in the weather. On that very evening there was heavy rain which continued for the best part of eighteen hours. And by Friday lunchtime a big question-mark had come over the river: how much extra water was it carrying?

I was unable to stand the suspense, wanting to see for myself just what the conditions were like, so I took a ride along to the venue on the Friday at about 1pm. And I was somewhat relieved to find that the increase in water level was only about four inches. It could have been a lot worse, although there was a nasty colour entering the match course mid-way along from a brook sited on the far bank.

The only thing now was to hope that the water levelled out. Given dry weather for the next eighteen hours there could well be an improvement by Saturday morning.

However, the social activities surrounding the world event were now getting under way and it was time for us to don our England blazers and make our way to Birmingham's Grand Hotel where a civic reception was being given for all the participating teams.

This was to be followed by the crucial meeting of the England camp when Stan Smith would announce who was to fill the dreaded position of reserve.

This was going to be a difficult decision for Stan because all members of the squad had enjoyed a certain amount of success at both the Championship venue and in big open events on the river during the preceding few weeks.

However, when the announcement did come it was one of the new signings, Max Winters, a close colleague of mine, who was omitted. We then got together and discussed last-minute tactics for what was going to be a very testing three hours of team fishing.

The next morning was match day and all our thoughts on the way to the venue were centred on the possible condition of the river. We disembarked from the coach and covered the 300 or 400 yards across the Luddington meadows to the water to find that a further deterioration had unfortunately taken place.

There had been a further rise of four or five inches, quickening the pace and adding to the colour. Some swims looked to be quite fishable but others certainly looked in a very poor state indeed. Bites here would be at a premium.

As we waited to know our respective sections we were surrounded by batteries of cameras and television crews. It made it extremely difficult to gain just a few seconds of peace to assess the deterioration in the river.

Eventually Stan Smith appeared to tell us our allotted sections: 'A' section John Dean, 'B' Kevin Ashurst, 'C' Dave Thomas, 'D' myself, and 'F' Tony Scott.

We made our way to our pegs, not short of helpers, and had to wait for the first maroon, at 9.55am, which signalled permission for us to enter our fishing grounds and start putting our tackle together. A second maroon would sound an hour later, when feeding of the swims could commence, and then five minutes after this, at 11am hooks could be baited and battle begin.

On entering my fishing ground I was very disappointed to see that the pace of the river was quite fast down the near margin, along my stick-float line. And I was both surprised and additionally disappointed to note that a large overhanging willow tree had been removed only the previous afternoon from its position three yards down the swim.

I could not convince myself that this removal would not damage the swim, and it made me all the more anxious to get started in the hope of catching one or two fish, and so allay my fears.

Across river near the far bank there appeared to be a deadwater sanctuary where fish could lie while the river was pushing through so strongly. Experience of the stretch told me that this piece of water would be littered with pandock beds, with very few areas of clear water.

But it would be worth making a cast into this area from time to time in the hope of dropping into a weed-free spot, knowing that the resident chub, if they were there, would accept the bait almost immediately as I had found out during practice.

This was just as well for within a matter of twenty seconds or so, the fast midstream current, helped by a downstream wind, would drag the float from this point and make it behave in a totally unrealistic manner.

Eventually we were given the signal to start feeding, and in no time at all there were dozens of orange-sized balls of bait—clay/biscuit/meal/bread and various other ingredients—zooming to different parts of the river.

The large crowd could be heard chanting as each ball left the hands of the many continental competitors, as if a uniform counting exercise were being carried out.

All I could do—and I imagine the other England men were performing likewise—was to fire an occasional pouchful of maggots to the far margin, and toss a few baits down the near edge, as if to mark time. Willy Russell, the Irish team member pegged immediately above me, did exactly the same. This was somewhat comforting, since at least I had the peg upstream of me completely free of this bombardment.

The next five minutes quickly expired, and with my tackle perfected during the previous hour, when all adjustments and shotting capacities can be completed quite legally under World Championship rules, I kicked off with a stick float, slowing it down to about a third of the current speed, five feet out from the bank.

After fifteen minutes I struck at a slight indication registered by the float, and on retrieving the tackle found a silver scale on the hook. This gave me mixed feelings for I am sure that in a less-important match a foul-hooked fish would have arrived at the net. But at least it told me that there were fish in the area. However, would they feed?

Nearly half an hour went by using this particular method, and I was a bit disappointed at the lack of early response. So I decided to make a challenge across to the far-bank swim.

Disappointment is plainly seen on the faces of the England team after finishing second in the 1981 World Championships – another near miss! (*Angler's Mail*)

After another ten minutes there was a slight dip of the float—a minnow had taken my large bronze maggot. Though normally cursed by English match anglers, I was glad to see that fish.

On a day when a dry net meant twenty-one penalty points, one more than the number of competing teams, this tiny minnow was worth at least a point, even if I finished last in the section.

Another two minnows followed during the next twenty minutes and then after no further response for quite some time I returned to the stick float. But here again I could not get a bite.

During the last hour of the match I had to keep convincing myself that I was correct to keep trying one method or the other and hope against hope that a fish would fall for my hookbait.

But the time slipped away, the penultimate maroon sounded indicating that only five more fishing minutes remained. But I couldn't possibly put more effort into the match as I had been working flat out for every second.

When the end came, I stood in utter disbelief trying to recall any occasion when I stood on the banks of this river during the month of September with as little as three minnows to show at the end of a contest.

Had I not won the Ladbroke Super only a fortnight earlier with three pounds to spare against a field of top nationally known anglers? It was indeed difficult, if not impossible, to take in.

I didn't even want to face the crowd. But eventually the scales arrived at my peg, and I must admit the news was more encouraging than I had hoped. I couldn't accept the fact that anyone else in my section could possibly have less than three minnows, yet already, I was told, there were five completely dry nets, and another two catches less than my own.

I eventually finished thirteenth out of the twenty anglers in my section, not a position I was proud of but certainly one I was willing to settle for with such a lowly catch.

When I saw Tony Scott, my team colleague in the downstream section, he had had a similar gruelling time, perhaps worse than I had experienced; from the pegs below him fish had been caught with seemingly comparative ease throughout the three hours!

At this point, Tony feared that he might finish as low as eighteenth in his section. But on the other hand, Dave Thomas had landed over ten pounds, an exceptional weight on the day, top catch in the match and, of course, a section winner.

Kevin Ashurst had finished third in his group with a brace of chub, losing four other fish during the match. And John Dean, from what was described as a 'no hope' peg, had produced another third best in his section with a handful of chub to confirm what a truly great angler he is.

Assembled in the presentation area, it quickly became obvious that the main danger to an England victory, France, had stormed home with some terrific performances, executed with their pole-and-bloodworm tactics so well suited to the badly discoloured, hard-running river.

Early assessments of our position put us anywhere between second and fifth.

When all the working-out was completed, a multitude of cameras waited to greet the 1981 World Champions. As predicted France mounted the rostrum as winners with a total points tally of twenty-five.

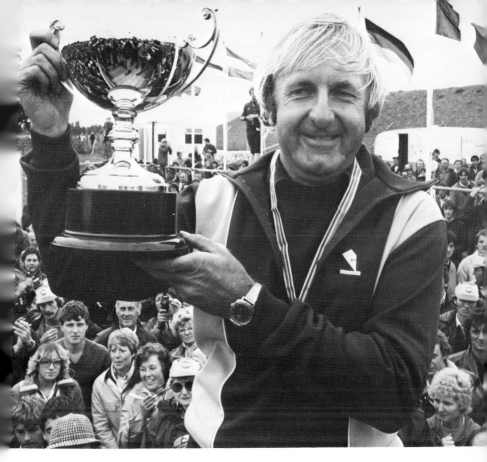

Dave Thomas with the World Championship trophy he won at Luddington in 1981 (*Angler's Mail*)

It was with mixed feelings that we heard second place had gone to England, six points behind France. This indicated to both Tony Scott—who, incidentally, gained a far better section position of eleventh than he could have hoped for with one dace and one gudgeon—and myself that one reasonable fish would have been sufficient to complete the job for England. In my case it would have needed to weigh only nine ounces for a World Champion's medal.

The result demonstrated that angling, in common with other sports, when followed with enthusiasm and passion, can lift its followers to the highest level of exultation, but at times like this, a once-in-a-lifetime occasion, it can also drop them to the depths of despair.

It was perhaps some consolation for England when the following day Dave Thomas further enhanced his impeccable record on the Warwickshire Avon. In atrocious conditions, even worse than in the team match the previous day, he managed to capture three fish and take the world individual crown from what must rate as the worst peg ever to win the title. Dave was destined to win the honour—truly deserved after his fine team performance—and to become a very worthy World Champion.